# SOUNDS MUSICAL

**Pauline Adams**

A Music Course for Key Stage 2 (7–11 years)

## Teacher's Resource Book

Music Department
Oxford University Press

## OXFORD
UNIVERSITY PRESS

Great Clarendon Street, Oxford OX2 6DP, England
198 Madison Avenue, New York, NY10016, USA

Oxford University Press is a department of the University of Oxford.
It furthers the University's aim of excellence in research, scholarship,
and education by publishing worldwide in

Oxford  New York
Auckland  Bangkok  Buenos Aires  Cape Town  Chennai
Dar es Salaam  Delhi  Hong Kong  Istanbul  Karachi  Kolkata
Kuala Lumpur  Madrid  Melbourne  Mexico City  Mumbai  Nairobi
São Paulo  Shanghai  Taipei  Tokyo  Toronto

Oxford is a registered trade mark of Oxford University Press
in the UK and in certain other countries

© Pauline Adams 1997

Reprinted with corrections 1999

10  9  8  7  6  5

British Library Cataloguing Publication Data available.

Teacher's Book ISBN 0 19 3209756
Pupils' set (Pink, Green, and Purple Books) ISBN 0 19 320976 4

*Acknowledgements:*

Illustrations by Juliet Breese, Anna Jupp, Sarah John, Jenny Mumford,
Wladek Szechter, Alex and Peter Tucker

Music engraved by Woodrow Edition

Photographs: Front cover ZEFFA; p.32 (top) Centre George Pompidou,
Paris/© ADAGP Paris and DACS, London 1997, Yellow-Red-Blue by Kandinsky;
(bottom) *Heroic Strokes of the Bow* (Heroische Bogenstriche) by Paul Klee 1938;
coloured paste on newspaper on dyed cotton fabric, 28 3/4 x 20 7/8"
(73 x 52.7cm.); The Museum of Modern Art, New York; photograph © 1996
The Museum of Modern Art, New York; p.70 (top) Hutchinson Picture Library,
(bottom) Navras Records; p.80 ZEFA; p.82 ZEFA; p.94 Cristina Eaton;
p.96 (top) Hutchinson Picture Library, (bottom) Navras Records;
p.100 Barnabys; p.112 Stripsody © Cathy Berberian; p.126 ZEFA.

*The publishers wish to thank the following for permission to reproduce copyright material:*

*Our Friend the Central Heating* Page 50: © 1990 John Foster, included by permission
of the author; 'Bagpipe music' p 62 © 1940 by Hawkes & Son (London) Ltd.,
reproduced by permission of Boosey & Hawkes Music Publishers Ltd.

*The World* by Donald Peters Page 86: every effort has been made to trace
the copyright holder of this poem, but without success; the publishers
will be grateful for information in order to rectify this omission at the next printing.

*Night Mail* by W. H. Auden Page 142: included by permission of the Post Office
Film and Video Library.

The publishers would like to thank Maxwell Pryce
for help with copy-editing.

The author would like to thank the following for their help:
Joanne Brooke, Chinese music specialist for the song *Bamboo flute*;
Judith Burden for general primary advice; Yvonne Browne
for help with editing and proof-reading; Sarah Herschel
and Jan Holdstock for original music and songs; Brendon McCarthy
and the pupils of Stoke Newington School, London.

Designed and typeset by Alex Tucker, Holbrook Design, Oxford

# Contents

CONTENTS

# Introduction

The teaching of music at Key Stage 2 should build on a balanced music curriculum planned and taught at Key Stage 1. Musical experiences should be practical and involve the skills of performing, composing and listening.

The purpose of SOUNDS MUSICAL is to enable teachers of children aged 7-11 to cover the music curriculum in an accessible, structured and relevant way.

The activities are often open-ended enough to allow children to bring their own experiences and skills to their music-making whilst at the same time providing a secure framework to ensure building progression into the learning.

*The components of the course*
Teacher's Resource Book
Three Pupils' Books (*The Pink Book*, *The Green Book*, and *The Purple Book*)
Recording pack (either two CDs or two cassettes)

## How to use the course

The main part of the Teacher's Book is divided into 24 projects, which can be used in any order, and each of which has a particular musical focus. The order in which they are undertaken will depend on the teacher's knowledge of his or her pupils' abilities and previous musical experience. However, the order of the projects progresses from those requiring the level of experience that could be expected from a child who has followed a balanced music curriculum through Key Stage 1 to those requiring the levels of knowledge, skills, and understanding which every child is entitled to have acquired as s/he approaches the end of Key Stage 2.

Some projects contain tasks which are weighted towards learning, practising and developing particular skills, whilst others are more open-ended, giving children opportunities to bring their own creativity, ideas and skills to their music.

Each project has two or three units of work which develop its musical focus. The division of each unit into three or four activities provides natural breaks within it, allowing the teacher to plan short sessions of work (perhaps covering just one activity) or longer sessions covering the whole unit.

Each activity has a set of icons which indicate whether it is for pairs, groups or the whole class, and also which areas of National Curriculum requirements are its main focus:

 indicates an activity for pairs

 indicates an activity for groups

 indicates an activity for the whole class

Activities headed by this icon broadly cover performance using instruments, and assume other factors such as control of sounds and awareness of audiences.

 This indicates that a listening piece is included in the activity, which will of course entail the discussion that is an essential part of appraisal.

 These activities cover the requirements both of singing and making body sounds, as well as other uses of the voice.

 This usually indicates the discussion that precedes a composition project, and the discussion of work in progress.

 These activities cover composing in response to various stimuli, and communication of ideas.

Naturally, most of the activities will include elements of all these aspects of the curriculum: the icons are just a quick and handy reference to the main aspects covered.

Many units finish with an extension activity, which is optional and may be suitable for selected group work. There are also short tasks in the Pupils' Books, suitable for individuals, pairs, or small groups.

The units are not given a timings, as each school's overall timetabling or classroom-based timetabling will determine the amount of time available for music, and how it is to be organized. For example, some teachers will organise small-group work with a whole class, whereas others will timetable it into their daily plan, so that perhaps only one or two groups are working on their music at a time.

It may not be possible, or desirable, to cover an entire unit of work in one session. Both teachers and children may bring a number of new ideas to the sessions, which the children may then wish to develop and refine. In order to do this, they will need time to practise their music.

**A brief description of each of the units, the relevant Pupils' Book tasks, the background to recorded material, and cross-curriculum links can be found on pages 8–27.**

### The Pupils' Books

These are an essential part of the scheme, as they provide:

*   The words and melody for all the songs.

*   A stimulus for discussion, and a source of ideas to spark off compositional and performance ideas in class lessons.

*   Visual and textual information for the units of work and for cross-curriculum projects.

*   A number of tasks which will engage children as independent learners. The tasks are related to the projects, and provide opportunities for partner and small-group work.

*   An exciting resource for the library and music corner,

### The recordings

These contain performances of all the songs used in the book, often in more than one version to help the children to learn them. Where possible, it is preferable that teachers use the recordings to learn the songs themselves, in order to sing them and teach them to the class. But the recordings alone, with their instrumental accompaniments, will provide a valuable resource for the children.

There are also short listening extracts, which are an integral part of most of the units. Background information for each piece can be found on pages 8–27, but teachers ought to bear in mind that children's appraisal of music should be encouraged spontaneously, without necessarily informing them immediately of any other information.

The resource box for each unit includes space [     ] for the teacher to insert cassette counter numbers.

# *Layout of each unit*

Project title
and number

Unit title
and number

Activity box

Resource box
for the unit:
(what you need
to get started)

Key vocabulary
(**bold** words
are defined in
the Glossary
page 158)

Previous
experience
required to
undertake the
unit

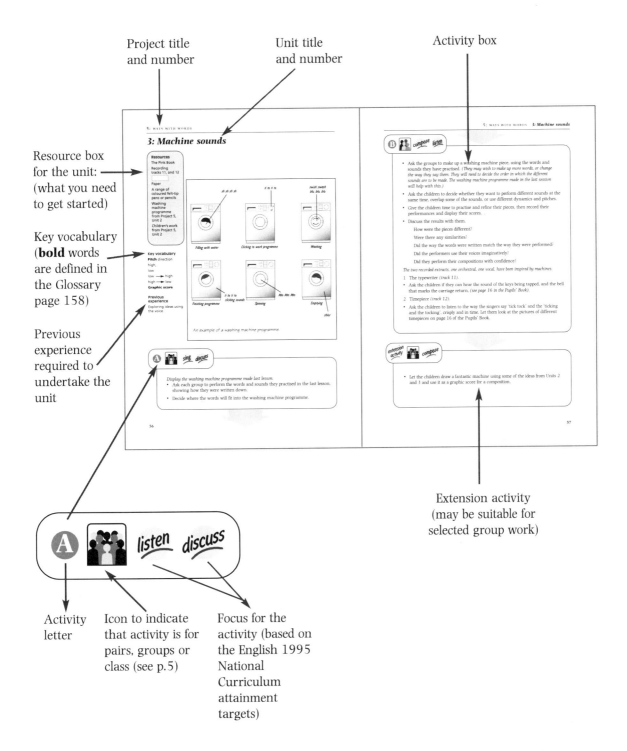

Activity
letter

Icon to indicate
that activity is for
pairs, groups or
class (see p.5)

Focus for the
activity (based on
the English 1995
National
Curriculum
attainment
targets)

Extension activity
(may be suitable for
selected group work)

# Background notes on the projects

## 1: The long and the short of it

### 1. Exploring sounds

Investigating sound through experimenting with instruments.
Controlling sound by using a range of techniques.

**TASK (pairs; *The Pink Book*, p.1)**

Further experimenting with exploring sound and instrumental playing techniques.
Passing on information and presenting ideas to others using clearly drawn and written instructions.

### 2. Exploring and scoring

Inventing clear symbols to represent long, short and continuous sounds.
Composing a graphic score.

**TASK (groups; *The Pink Book*, p.3)**

Performing a graphic score.

### 3. Exploring and recording

Creating and performing a graphic composition.
Listening to and appraising group compositions.

**TASK (pairs or small groups; *The Pink Book*, pp.4 and 5)**

Using art work, both well-known and their own, as a stimulus for music making.

### *Cross-curriculum links*

Factual writing
Art

## 2: Feeling the pulse

### 1. Doo-be doo (track 1)

Singing a song, clapping both on and off the beat.
Composing a short piece with a steady beat, and varying dynamics by using vocal
and body sounds.
Recording their music by creating a graphic score.

**TASK (pairs; *The Pink Book*, p.6)**

Practising on- and off-beat patterns from notation.
Creating other sounds for the rhythms.

***LISTENING PIECE***

*One Love*, Bob Marley and the Wailers (track 2)
This reggae song illustrates clearly the off-beat patterns which are the essence of this style
of music. The bass guitar can be heard playing on the first beat of each bar whilst
the rhythm guitar can be heard strumming off-beat chords.

### 2. Patterns

Rehearsing, refining and performing compositions.
Listening to and appraising their own and others' music.
Extending compositions.

**TASK (individuals or groups; *The Pink Book*, p.7)**

Playing a graphic score.

***LISTENING PIECE***

*Walking the Dog*, Sarah Herschel (track 3)
This music has been written using a computer programme. There are four distinct sounds
which are heard over a repeated bass line. The pupils' score shows clearly the changing
order of the sounds, and the 'dog bark' surprise ending.

# 3: Grouping the beat

### 1.     Threes, fours and fives
Playing different beat groupings.
Listening to and identifying different beat groupings.
**TASK (individuals or pairs; *The Pink Book*, p.8 and 9)**
Recognizing patterns and establishing a beat.
***LISTENING PIECES***
*a. 'Minuet' from Music for the Royal Fireworks, George Frideric Handel (1685–1759)
(track 4)*

The minuet, originally a fashionable triple-time dance in the 17th century, was used
by many composers in larger works in the 18th century. Handel was commissioned
to write a suite of pieces for a fireworks display, in Green Park, London, in 1749.
He used the minuet to create a grand finale to his piece. Page 8 of *The Pink Book*
shows a contemporary print of the event, which was attended by over 12,000 people.

*b. 'March' from the opera Love of Three Oranges,  Serge Prokofiev (1891–1953) (track 5)*
A steady four-beat pulse is heard throughout this lively march, which is played by a full
symphony orchestra.  In this extract a short introduction gradually gets louder, and
then trumpets are heard heralding the main melody of the march. Contrasting music
is played in between repetitions of the melody, and the march reaches its conclusion
with the whole orchestra playing to a steady four-beat pulse. The abrupt ending is
created by the last note being sounded on the third beat of the bar. Percussion plays
an important time-keeping role in the march, and the children should be able to
recognize the glockenspiel which permeates the orchestral texture.

*c. 'Mars, the bringer of war' from The Planets, Gustav Holst (1894–1934) (track 6)*
*The Planets* is Holst's most famous composition. It is a suite of orchestral pieces,
finished in 1916, and based on the seven planets known of at the time (Pluto was
not discovered until 1930). 'Mars' is also the name of the Roman god of war.
The main feature of this piece is the relentlessly powerful and war-like five-beat
ostinato. It reflects the time at which it was written (during the First World War),
and also Holst's interest in astrology and horoscopes.

### 2.     Transforming the pulse
Composing and notating a short piece using different beat groupings.
**TASK (individuals or groups; *The Pink Book*, p.10)**
Using different inputs and outputs.

## *Cross-curriculum links*
Maths
History

## 4: Answers and echoes

**1.  Hill an' gully (track 7)**
Singing a song in 'call and response' style.
Imitating 'call and response' patterns from the song.
**TASK (individuals or groups; *The Pink Book*, p.11)**
Identifying and clapping rhythmic and melodic notated patterns from the song.

**2.  Call and response**
Creating and playing an accompaniment to a song.
Composing a short composition based on 'call and response' ideas.
**TASK (individuals/pairs; *The Pink Book*, p.11)**
See Unit 1.

**3.  Echo song**
*Version 1 - two voices (track 8)*
*Version 2 - drum and tambourine (track 9)*
Singing a song which uses repetition and overlapping sounds.
Experimenting with imitation, overlapping sounds and echo effects.
**TASK (individuals or groups; *The Pink Book*, p.12)**
Further work on echoes.

*Cross-curriculum links*
Science

## 5: Ways with words

**1.  The big machine (track 10)**
Singing a song which includes onomatopoeia.
Inventing and vocalizing onomatopoeic word sounds.

**2.  Central heating**
Exploring words and vocal sounds in imaginative ways.
**TASK (individuals or groups; *The Pink Book*, pp.14 and 15)**
Ordering a sequence of pictures. Interpreting machine ideas using voices.

**3.  Machine sounds**
Composing a vocal piece in response to a visual stimulus.
Listening to and appraising their own and others' music.
**TASK (individuals or groups; *The Pink Book*, p.16)**
Making lists of things which measure time.
The object the children are asked to identify is an antique (but hi-tech!) desk tidy for pens, ink, etc.
***LISTENING PIECES***
*a. 'The Typewriter', Leroy Anderson (1908–75) (track 11)*
The American composer Leroy Anderson used an orchestra to create the sounds of an old-fashioned typewriter. Using the picture on page 16 of *The Pink Book*, explain to the children how the typist fed the paper onto the roller, pressed the keys to type the words, and how at the end of each line a bell rang so that the typist could move the paper on for the next line. Discuss the difference between this and using a computer to write letters. Ask the children to listen for the sound of the keys being tapped, the bell, and the sound of the roller moving the paper on.

*b. 'Time Piece', Paul Patterson (born 1947) (track 12)*
This vocal piece by the English composer Paul Patterson is performed by five male voices. The use of rhythm and onomatopoeic words such as 'ticking and a-tocking' are intended to convey the sound of a ticking wrist-watch. Ask the children to lightly tap out the speed of the ticking watch. The style of the singing in this section of the piece can also be described as light.

### Cross-curriculum links
English

## 6: Rhythmic vocals

### 1. Monkey chant
Listening to and appraising one particular style of vocal music.
Performing and keeping an independent part in a vocal rhythmic chant.
**TASK (individuals or groups; *The Pink Book*, p.18)**
Using and memorizing a pentatonic scale.
*LISTENING PIECE*
*'Kecak', Balinese Monkey Chant (track 13)*
Kecak (pronounced 'ketjak') is a style of vocal composition which is sung in Indonesia, usually by a chorus of men. It accompanies the *Ramayana* epic, in which the Princess Sita is rescued from the demon king Ravana by an army of monkeys (the story is told on p.17 of *The Pink Book*). The chorus imitate the chattering sounds of the monkeys, using interlocking vocal rhythms. In the recorded extract, a sung melody accompanies the chant. A time-keeper can be heard voicing the pulse (the speed of which constantly changes) above the texture created by the melody and the chant.

### 2. Gamelan
Adding a simple melodic accompaniment to a vocal rhythmic chant.
Learning and using a numbered form of notation.
Listening to and appraising an authentic Gamelan composition.
*LISTENING PIECE*
*Gamelan 'Royal', Traditional Javanese (track 14)*
This particular piece of gamelan music was traditionally played in the royal palaces of Java, Indonesia. The music is played in a loud, confident style. The instruments playing the interlocking melodies characteristic of this style of music are all made of metal. The drum plays an important part, as the player is responsible for giving various signals for musical changes, including speeding up and slowing down.

The piece begins with an introduction played on the bonang (a set of small gongs) followed by the drum. As a large gong is sounded, a melody enters which is then repeated a number of times. The drum and a wood block control the gradual slowing down of this melody. When the music has settled in its new slow tempo, the melody line changes, and the bonang decoration can be clearly heard.

The piece uses a seven-note scale, called a Pelog. The sound this Indonesian scale creates may be unfamiliar to the ears of some children. Pointing out that instruments are tuned differently within various musical traditions around the world may help children to listen with more informed ears.

### Cross-curriculum links
English and drama

## 7: Discovering drones

### 1. Droning on

Listening to and naming some of the instruments which can produce a drone.
Experimenting and creating drones on classroom instruments.

**LISTENING PIECES**

*Drones*

These short listening extracts give example of four different kinds of instruments which play drones. The Indian tambura (track 15) can be heard setting up the drone at the beginning of this extract, but is soon joined by the sitar, which is heard playing a descending scale. The drone continues as the sitar begins to develop the alap (see Glossary page 158). The bagpipe extract (track 17) is of an Irish Uillean (pronounced 'ill-yin') pipe. *Uillean* means 'elbow' in Gaelic, and in this type of pipe the bag is operated by the elbow. Information about the French hurdy-gurdy (track 18), the Australian didjeridu (track 16), the Indian tambura (track 15), and the history of the bagpipe can be found on pages 20 and 21 of *The Pink Book.*

### 2. Round and round

*Version 1 - (track 19)*
*Version 2 - with coda (track 20)*
Singing a song with a drone accompaniment.

### 3. Bach and Bartók

Improvising over a drone.
Listening and appraising their own and other's music.

**TASK (individuals or groups; *The Pink Book*, p.24)**
Unusual ways of creating drones.

**LISTENING PIECES**

*a. 'Gavotte II (ou la Musette)' from English Suite No.3, J. S. Bach (1685–1750) (track 21)*
This dance for harpsichord conveys the feel of a musette (a type of bagpipe) by having one note in the bass (left hand) played the whole way through. The harpsichord was the most commonly played keyboard instrument at the time Bach was composing. Today this piece is often played on the piano.

*b. 'Bagpipe' from Mikrokosmos volume 5, Béla Bartók (1881–1945) (track 22)*
Bartók uses the pitches G and D to accompany most of this piano piece. It reflects his love of Hungarian folk music. Bartók divides the drone notes, using the G and D alternately, and as the piece progresses, he takes advantage of the wide pitch range of the piano to extend the pitch of the drone to the G and D an octave lower.

### Cross-curriculum links

Science
History

## 8: Building a chord

### 1    Ring out!

*Version 1 - unison (track 23)*
*Version 2 - round (track 24)*
Singing a round. Constructing and playing a chord.

**TASK (pairs; *The Green Book*, p.1)**

Creating an accompaniment to *Ring out!*

### 2.    Tuneful chords

Accompanying a song with a chord.
Experimenting and composing using chord patterns.

**TASK (individuals or groups; *The Green Book*, p.2)**

Following notation while listening to the bugle call.

***LISTENING PIECE***

*Bugle call (track 25)*

This call is a cavalry call used by the American army. The children may have heard this or similar calls in 'Western' films.

### *Cross-curriculum links*

History

## 9: Melody ways

### 1.    Oats and beans

*Version 1 - scale going down (track 26)*
*Version 2 - scale going up (track 27)*
*Version 3 - two voices (track 28)*
Singing a song with a descending scale.
Experimenting with different ways of playing a scale.

### 2.    Raga moods

Experimenting with playing a scale using long and short sounds.
Listening to and appraising an extract of Indian music which uses long
and short sounds.
Creating a scale and composing a short piece which uses long and short sounds.

***LISTENING PIECE***

*Raga 'Jait' (track 29)*

This raga is played on an Indian flute by Pandit Hari Prasad.
The music of South-East Asia (which includes India, Bangladesh and Pakistan)
uses many different series of notes (scales) called 'rags' or 'ragas'. As well as having
its own set of notes, each raga is also considered to have a special mood or character
making it suitable to be played at certain times of day or on certain occasions.
Ragas serve as a basis for the performers' improvisation, and the pieces of music thus
created are also called ragas. At the beginning of a piece of Indian classical music
there is usually an introduction, called 'alap', which is played slowly and thoughtfully,
and is a way of exploring the mood of the raga.

There is no beat in this music. It is free and expressive, allowing the player to explore the mood in a creative and personal way.

This extract is from the opening of the raga. In the particular performance from which this extract is taken, Hari Prasad played the notes of the raga, ascending and descending, before then starting to play the alap (or introduction). The alap alone lasted 37 minutes. The mood of this raga is devotional, and it is also the only North-Indian raga which can be played either in the morning or evening. Point out to the children how well-suited the flute is to playing the long notes and sliding pitches.

### Cross-curriculum links
Geography

# 10: Pentatonic patterns

### 1. Zum gali gali
*Version 1 - unison (track 30)*
*Version 2 - unison and ostinato (track 31)*
Singing a song written in the pentatonic scale.
Accompanying a song with a sung ostinato.
Improvising over an ostinato using the pentatonic scale.

### 2. Repeated patterns
Listening to and appraising a recorded example of an African composition based on pentatonic ostinato patterns.
Playing and singing independent parts within an ostinato composition.
**LISTENING PIECE**

*Ugandan balafon players (track 32)*

The balafon players in this extract are playing interlocking repeated patterns. Children who play the xylophone will appreciate the skill required to fit the different parts together, and to keep in time when repeating a pattern many times. There is a picture, and more information about the balafon on page 5 of *The Green Book*.

### 3. Patterns in performance
Composing, structuring and playing pentatonic ostinato pieces which include a range of dynamics.
Listening to and appraising the finished compositions.

### Cross-curriculum links
Geography

## 11: Mood music

### 1. Sounds from junk

Using 'junk' instruments as a musical resource.
Exploring the different sounds produced by a range of 'junk' instruments.
Experimenting with dynamics, tempo, timbre and texture using a range
of 'junk' instruments.

**TASK (individuals or groups; *The Green Book*, p.6)**
Experimenting with different beaters.

*LISTENING PIECES*

*a. 'Noye's Fludde', Benjamin Britten (1913–76) (track 33)*

This short extract is from *Noye's Fludde*, Britten's children's opera based on one of the Chester
Miracle plays. The composer wrote parts for amateur players to join the orchestra. They are
asked to create the sound of rain drops by striking different sizes of drinking mugs with
wooden spoons. The cups are hung up to create a scale. The children can listen to the tune
they make, which is accompanied by strings and piano.

*b. 'Yellow Bird', Norman Luboff (track 34)*

This is a steel band version of a well-known Caribbean song. The steel pan originated
in Trinidad to play at Carnival time, but has become very popular in Britain.

### 2. Creating a mood

Using musical contrasts as a way of exploring timbre and texture.
Creating music from a given stimulus.

**TASK (pairs or groups; *The Green Book*, pp.8 and 9)**
Responding in words and music to a visual stimulus.

*LISTENING PIECES*

*a. 'The Storm', from the suite The Sea, Frank Bridge (1879–1941) (track 35)*

This orchestral piece conjures up the wind, rain and raging sea during a storm. Bridge taught
composition to the composer Benjamin Britten, who later wrote his own *Four Sea Interludes*,
including a storm piece, for his opera *Peter Grimes*.

*b. 'Winter', from The Four Seasons, Antonio Vivaldi (1678–1741) (track 36)*

This popular composition is scored for strings and keyboard. A special bowing technique
is used to produce a sharp shivering effect as the different instruments enter: first the cellos,
then the violas, and finally the violins. The solo violinist plays a lot of trills, which add
to the 'shiver' factor.

*c. 'The Lark Ascending', Ralph Vaughan Williams (1872–1958) (track 37)*

Much of the music written by the composer Vaughan Williams was influenced by the tradition
of English folk song. This piece, written for solo violin and small orchestra, evokes the sounds
of the English countryside.

The lark, represented by the solo violin, plays gently rising melodic phrases, soaring upwards.
The children could discuss whether they think the violin is a suitable instrument to represent
the skylark.

*d. 'Desert Music', Steve Reich (born 1936) (track 38)*

This piece is a setting of poems by the American poet William Carlos Williams. The music
was completed in 1983, and a combination of voices and instruments can be heard in this
extract. The piece is based on repeated ostinatos, and is composed in a minimalist style, that
builds on repeated short fragments of music. The children should focus on the atmosphere
created by the piece and describe in words their individual responses.

### Cross-curriculum links
English

# 12: City music

### 1. The quiet city

Listening and responding to music which creates a particular atmosphere.
Listening to and analysing ways in which composers use dynamics, tempo, timbre and texture to create different atmospheres.

*LISTENING PIECE*

*'Quiet City', Aaron Copland (1900–90) (track 39)*

In his composition *Quiet City*, the American composer Aaron Copland creates the tranquil atmosphere of empty city streets, a tranquillity which will soon be broken as the hustle and bustle and tensions of daily life emerge with the dawn of another day.

The piece is scored for cor anglais (woodwind family), trumpet (brass family), and violins, violas, cellos and double basses (string family). The composer uses only one cor anglais and one trumpet, which are at times heard playing single melodic lines. The strings often play long, sustained sounds. This sparing use of instrumentation gives the piece the uncluttered and spacious texture required in order to create the atmosphere of a quiet city.

### 2. The wakening city

Exploring ways of linking two musically contrasting pieces.
Listening to and appraising two contrasting pieces.

*LISTENING PIECE*

*'Ionisation', Edgar Varése (1883–1965) (track 40)*

The French-born composer Varése uses very different instruments in his piece *Ionisation*, and it is stylistically in total contrast to Copland's *Quiet City*.

The piece is written for thirteen percussion players, playing thirty-eight instruments! Each player has a number of instruments to play, and must be ready to do so. The instruments are laid out for easy access and the player must pick them up and put them down quietly after playing.

In this piece there are no sustained strings or long melodic lines, but a chaotic sounding of a whole battery of percussion instruments (including piano and glockenspiel), playing short rhythmic phrases. The only long, sustained sound is that of two sirens. Their sounds are those of disturbance and urgency as they glide up and down in pitch, evoking the sound of a police car or ambulance rushing to an emergency.

### 3. Creation city

Extending and refining compositions.
Listening to and appraising finished compositions.

**TASK (pairs or groups; *The Green Book*, p.13)**

Creating music based on a picture.

### *Cross-curriculum links*

English - poetry

## 13: Sounds extended

### 1. Trying them out

Controlling dynamics and tempo.

*LISTENING PIECES*

*a. Overture from 'The Barber of Seville', Gioachino Rossini (1792–1868) (track 41)*

The Italian composer Rossini is very famous for the crescendos in his music. This one lasts for about 50 seconds. The music gradually gets louder, but is also built up by adding more instruments throughout the crescendo. The music starts with only the woodwind and strings playing, with brass instruments and percussion added later. The impression of the music speeding up is created by fitting more and more notes into the beat.

*b.' Night', Chinese percussion music (track 42)*

This extract features a solo passage played on a drum. The children should be asked to listen to the way the drummer controls both dynamics and tempo. The player has developed a very good stick technique to be able to play this music.

### 2. Time lines

Organizing and notating sounds within a time line to create a short composition. Listening to and appraising the effects of combining sound and silence within a composition.

### 3. Sounds together

Conducting and improvisation.
Listening to and appraising contemporary percussion compositions.

**TASK (pairs or small groups; *The Green Book*, p.17)**

Playing a graphic score.

*LISTENING PIECES*

*a. 'The Road is Wider than Long', Lindsay Cooper (track 43)*

The composer Lindsay Cooper is one of a number of women who are now making a significant contribution to British musical life. This piece was written in 1991. The opening uses solo instruments to create overlapping sounds. The instruments are used sparingly, and effectively create a very clear texture. The instruments played in this extract enter in the following order: kettledrum, keyboard, rainmaker, bass clarinet, woodblock and violin (which on first entering plays harmonics), Indian bells.

*b. 'Second Construction', John Cage (1912–92) (track 44)*

The American avant-garde composer John Cage was fascinated by the components of music, sound and silence. In this percussion piece he explores a range of techniques. This extract opens with a short two-note rhythmic phrase played on the glockenspiel, which is followed by a sustained sound on the tam-tam (a large gong). The glockenspiel plays a longer phrase using more notes, again answered by the tam-tam. The piece builds up in intensity as a different sound on the tam-tam introduces the piano (played in unusual ways, including on the strings inside) and the side drum. The glockenspiel enters again, using the ideas from its earlier longer phrase, and then on its final entry in the extract returns to the first two-note idea.

### Cross-curriculum links

Science

## 14: Talking drums

### Background information on drum notation

The drum performs a very important musical function in musical ceremonies and celebrations all over the world. In some societies it is regarded as a sacred instrument whose sounds connect with the spirit and demon worlds.

When players are not playing from written notation there is often the misconception that they are always improvising. In a number of drumming traditions they may, however, be using sophisticated mnemonic notation systems to identify required techniques and set rhythms. In the Middle East and North Africa, the mnemonic 'dhum' indicates a low sound, and 'tak' a high sound.

### The tabla

A mnemonic notation (or spoken drum language) is used in the Indian subcontinent by tabla players. The tabla are the most popular type of drum played in North India. A tabla player learns to produce a wide range of sounds by striking the pair of hand drums which make up the tabla on different parts of the skin, and with different parts of the hand. Each sound is given a mnemonic. 'Dha' and 'dhin' involve both drums being played at once, while 'ta' and 'tin' are sounds produced on the small drum only. The tabla player has to learn many different rhythm patterns called 'bols', which in Hindi means 'to speak'.

The Indian mnemonic sounds are not so far removed from the dhum and tak used in the Middle East. Both denote pitch as well as quality of sound.

### 1.　Dhum tak

Experimenting with techniques for producing differently pitched sounds on drums.
Learning a mnemonic notation specific to drumming in the Middle East.
Composing a short rhythmic sequence in a particular Middle-Eastern style .

**TASK (individuals; *The Green Book*, p.18)**

Playing a masmoudi rhythm.

***LISTENING PIECE***

*Traditional Egyptian drum rhythm (track 45)*

The particular rhythm on this track is called 'masmoudi', and is played on the darabuka (also known as tabla or dumbek), a goblet-style drum used across the Middle East and North Africa. This drum is single-headed and has a metal or pottery base.

The rhythm fits into an eight-beat cycle. The children should be able to hear the differently-pitched sounds created by using a combination of different hand techniques on specific areas of the drum skin. The repetition of the rhythm creates a fixed pattern of low and high sounds, in which the low-pitched sounds are always heard on beats one, two and five.

**2.** **Dha dhin dhin**

Listening to and appraising the range of different sounds which can be produced on a tabla.

Learning and memorizing a mnemonic notation specific to the Indian subcontinent.

*LISTENING PIECE*

*Tabla players, Calcutta, India (track 46)*

This is a 'field' recording of two amateur tabla players practising together. Here they are accompanied by a harmonium playing a simple repeating melody. It is important that the bols (spoken rhythm patterns) are committed to memory, and therefore an important part of the learning process is to speak the boles out loud before playing them.

Point out to the children that when performing on this instrument the player has to learn a complicated series of hand techniques, and also has to memorize many different set rhythm patterns.

*Cross-curriculum links*

Geography

## 15: Calypso time

**1.** **Panamam tombé (track 50)**

Singing a song composed in calypso style.
Clapping a basic calypso rhythm to accompany a song.

**2.** **Bongo rhythm**

Accompanying a song with a calypso-style rhythm on percussion.
Listening to and appraising a recorded extract which uses calypso-style rhythms.
Learning and playing chords to accompany a song composed in calypso style.

*LISTENING PIECE*

*'Jamaican Rumba', Arthur Benjamin (1893–1960), arr. Reginald Kell (track 51)*

The British composer Arthur Benjamin originally wrote this piece for two pianos. This arrangement is for clarinet and piano, and there is also an arrangement for orchestra. The piano accompaniment is written in the same calypso style which the children are required to practise for the accompaniment to the song 'Panamam tombé'. The rhythm is divided between the left and right hands, as is the bongo rhythm on page 21 of *The Green Book*.

The clarinet plays the melody over the piano accompaniment, which mainly sustains the same rhythm throughout. However, at one point in the piece the piano plays the second half of the melody in the bass, while the clarinet plays the first half of the melody at the same time.

*Cross-curriculum links*

Geography

## 16: Twos and threes

### 1. Rhythmic division

Practising and playing different beat-groupings at different tempos, written in grid notation.

Composing and notating a short, structured piece using different beat-groupings.

### 2. Cross-rhythm

Listening to and recognizing different rhythms both played and notated.

Learning and practising a chant which uses cross-rhythms.

**LISTENING PIECES**

*Cross-rhythm 1: grid 1 (track 52)*
*Cross-rhythm 2: grid 2 (track 53)*
*Cross-rhythm 3: grids 1 and 2 (track 54)*

The recorded extracts demonstrate cross-rhythmic effects, linked to the two grids as seen on page 157 of the Teacher's Book and page 22 of *The Green Book*.

The cross-rhythmic effect is produced by dividing the six-beat grids into accented groups of two and three beats. Different instrumental playing techniques also help to define the accents. Each of the two grids is first heard separately (tracks 52 and 53), and then in combination (track 54).

### 3. High life

Learning a song with a changing time signature.

Accompanying a song with a changing time signature.

**LISTENING PIECES**

*Version 1: voice and clapping (track 55)*
*Version 2: voice and drum (track 56)*
*Version 3: voice and instruments (track 57)*

### *Cross-curriculum links*

Maths

## 17: Exploring the voice

### 1.  Comic capers

Exploring and graphically notating vocal ideas.
Listening to and appraising a contemporary vocal composition.

### 2.  Comic strips

Directing, improvising and performing vocal ideas.
Composing and notating using vocal ideas.

**TASK (individuals or groups; *The Purple Book*, p.2)**

Making up titles for comic strips.

### 3.  Comic voices

Notating a graphic score which demonstrates the use of different dynamics and pitch.
Rehearsing, performing and appraising vocal compositions and scores.

***LISTENING PIECE***

*'Stripsody', Cathy Berberian (1925–83) (track 58)*

*Stripsody* was composed in 1966 by the American singer Cathy Berberian, based
on the words and sounds found in comic strips. All the sound effects in the
composition are produced with the voice.

The three lines of the score on page 112 of the Teacher's Book and page 3 of *The Purple
Book* represent low, medium and high pitches, and the spacing between the words
indicates timing.

### *Cross-curriculum links*

Language
Art and Graphics

## 18: Vocal messages

### 1 Chairs to mend (track 59)

Singing a three-part round based on street cries.
Listening to and appraising an extract of music composed using authentic street cries.

**LISTENING PIECE**

'The Cryes of London', Orlando Gibbons (1583–1625) (track 60)

This piece for five voices and five stringed instruments is based on actual street cries heard by the Elizabethan composer Gibbons. The different wares for sale are clearly heard, and are sung in a wide range of mixed voices. Other composers who were contemporaries of Gibbons also wrote compositions based on street cries.

### 2. Street cries

Composing music based on the theme of street cries.
Listening to and appraising a contemporary composition which uses the theme of street cries.

**LISTENING PIECE**

'Money, Penny' from 'Cries of London', Luciano Berio (born 1925) (track 61)

*Cries of London* was composed by the Italian composer Luciano Berio in 1976. These modern versions of old London street cries use imaginative and dramatic ways to convey the bustling scenes of a market, and the need to find novel ways of marketing goods. In 'Money, Penny', the repetition of the word 'money' gets to the heart of what trade is all about: money circulating round and round.

### Cross-curriculum links

History
Drama

## 19: Using chords

### 1. Drunken sailor

*Version 1: Unison (track 62)*
*Version 2: Two-part (track 63)*
Singing and analysing the structure of a simple song.
Learning and playing two different chords.

### 2. Playing with chords

Singing a song with a simple second part.
Accompanying a song with two different chords.

### 3. Three-chord trick

Learning and playing three different chords.
Listening to and identifying three chords played in a short sequence.
Composing and improvising over a chosen short chord sequence.

**TASK (individuals or pairs; *The Purple Book*, p.8)**

Following a line of notation while listening to an extract of music.

**LISTENING PIECE**

'Boogie bass', Sarah Herschel (track 64)

A catchy melody on the clarinet is accompanied by a bass line (on page 8 of *The Purple Book*). This 'walking' boogie-style line is based on the repetition of the three chords of G, C, and D major. The piano enters first playing the three chords, followed by the double bass, and finally the clarinet.

## 20: Clustering around

### 1. Creating clusters

Experimenting with the chromatic scale.
Creating clusters using the chromatic scale.

### 2. Exploding clusters

Experimenting with creating clusters using small and wide intervals.
Composing a cluster piece using pictures as a stimulus.

***LISTENING PIECE***

*Piece 5 from 'Klavierstücke', ('Piano Pieces'), Karlheinz Stockhausen (born 1928) (track 65)*

The German experimentalist composer Karlheinz Stockhausen wrote *Klavierstücke* in the early 1950s. The music is presented as separately written fragments, and the player is left to decide in which order they are to be played. This style of composing is known as chance composition.

The pianist uses a range of different and unusual playing techniques, such as pressing down piano keys silently to give added resonance to other pitched notes already sounding. The marked contrasts between sound and silence, long sustained notes juxtaposed by sudden movement (created by sharp changes in tempo), the use of the wide-ranging pitch of the piano, and the facility for creating 'bunches' of notes all help to inform the children of the range of cluster ideas which can be worked on in this unit.

## 21: Round up

### 1.  Sumer is icumin in

Listening to and appraising a round which has a sung ostinato accompaniment.
Singing and playing an ostinato.

**TASK (individuals or groups; *The Purple Book*, p.10)**

Looking at medieval English words.

***LISTENING PIECES***

*1. 'Sumer is icumin in', Anonymous 13th-century song*

This medieval song is thought to have been written down by a monk at Reading Abbey around the year 1240. The melody is possibly older still, but its origin is not really known. The piece is the only known six-part music written before the 15th century. The manuscript is displayed at the British Museum, it shows a Latin text as well as the more familiar English one, and also has instructions for performance.

*Version 1 (track 66):* The melody of the whole song, sung in medieval English.
*Version 2 (track 67):* The whole song, with a short, sung ostinato.
*Version 3 (track 68):* A performance by the Hilliard Ensemble.

There are six singers in version 3, and the song starts with the ostinato sung in canon by two singers, which continues throughout the piece. The introductory ostinato is followed by:

> the melody sung once through by one singer.
> the melody sung once through by two singers, as a round.
> the melody sung twice through, by four singers, as a round.

The ostinato finishes the performance.

### 2.  Rounds and ostinato

Singing a round and adding an ostinato accompaniment.
Improvising and performing a melody over an ostinato accompaniment.

***LISTENING PIECES***

*a. 'Sumer is icumin in', Version 4 (track 69)*

The whole song sung as a round with a recorder ostinato.

*b. 'A Spring Symphony', Benjamin Britten (1913–76) (track 70)*

The finale of this symphony (which is based on English seasonal poems) is a setting of *Sumer is icumin in*. It was written in 1949, and gives the children the opportunity to hear a twentieth-century version of the song.

### 3.  Rap on the move

Learning a piece composed in rap style.
Creating and performing an instrumental or rhythmic vocal accompaniment.

***LISTENING PIECE***

*'Rap on the move', Pauline Adams, arranged by pupils from Stoke Newington School, London.*

These two different versions of *Rap on the move* should provide the children with ideas for making their own arrangements. The first version (track 71) is accompanied by a bass ostinato and drum. The second version (track 72) uses vocal percussive sounds as an accompaniment.

### *Cross-curriculum links*

History
Language

## 22: Pentatonic melodies

### 1. Chinese numbers

Learning and using Chinese number notation.
Singing a Chinese song using numbered notation.

**LISTENING PIECE**

'Bamboo flute', Chinese folk song
*Version 1: The melody sung in numbers (track 73)*

### 2. Bamboo flute

Singing a Chinese song using an English transcription of the words.
Creating and playing an accompaniment in an appropriate style.

**LISTENING PIECES**

'Bamboo flute'
*Version 2: The song in Chinese and English (track 74)*
*Version 3: Instrumental version using a concert flute and yang qin (track 75)*

### *Cross-curriculum links*

Geography

## 23: Steam trains

### 1. Down the line

Listening to and identifying authentic recorded sounds of steam trains.
Imitating the sounds vocally and appraising through performance.

**LISTENING PIECES**

*Steam train and railway sound effects*

(i). *An express steam train passing by (track 76)*

The train is moving very fast. The sound gradually gets louder as it gets nearer,
and then quieter as it passes by and goes off into the distance. The rhythmic sound of
the wheels can be heard as they pass along the tracks (clickerty-clack; clickerty-clack).

(ii). *A local steam train starting out from the station (track 77)*

The train gives a whistle to signal that it is leaving. The 'chuff' sound of the steam is
heard as a steady pulse. (Ask the children to listen to the way the train gathers speed:
chuff-chuff-chuff-chuff . . . chuffa-chuffa-chuffa chuffa.)

(iii). *Trains in a marshalling yard shunting wagons (track 78)*

Ask the children to listen for the metallic clangs and clatters as the wagons are
uncoupled and coupled to assemble the trains. These sounds are heard as random and
do not form any particular rhythmic pattern.

(iv). *A large and busy station (track 79)*

The station announcer can be heard, but her voice is drowned out by the sound of a train arriving and squealing to a halt. Another train is then heard leaving the station.

(v). *Sounds heard inside an old, lever-operated signal box (track 80)*

There are several men working in the signal box, as it is a busy time with lots of trains passing by. The crash of levers being pulled can be heard, and bell codes are exchanged with other signal boxes along the line.

(vi). *A train waiting at the station with the fireman busy stoking up the boiler (track 81)*

The clang of a hammer and a coal shovel can be heard. The train whistles before it leaves the station.

## 2. Clickerty-chuff

Using steam-train rhythm words vocally and instrumentally.
Listening to recorded extracts of descriptive music.
**TASK (pairs; *The Purple Book*, p.17)**

Saying two-part rhythms in different ways.

### *LISTENING PIECES*

*a. 'Pacific 231', Arthur Honegger (1892–1955) (track 82)*

The French composer Arthur Honegger wrote *Pacific 231* in 1923. It is a descriptive piece written for a large symphony orchestra. (See a page of the score in *The Purple Book*, page 18.)

When interviewed about *Pacific 231*, Honegger said: 'The piece opens with the quiet breathing of the engine at rest, the straining at starting, the gradually increasing speed.' This extract is taken from the beginning of the piece. Allow the children to make their own responses to the music before discussing the composer's intentions.

Why '*Pacific 231*'? If the children look at the drawing of the engine on the front of Honegger's score (*The Purple Book*, page 18) they will see 2 small wheels followed by 3 large wheels, and then 1 wheel!

*b. 'Murder on the Orient Express', Richard Rodney Bennett (born 1936) (track 83)*

The English composer Richard Rodney Bennett has written music for a number of films. This is another example of descriptive composition. There are similarities between Honegger's and Bennett's musical intentions at the beginning of their pieces: Bennett also opens his piece with the train stationary, gathering steam for the beginning of the journey. The music speeds up into a fast waltz-style as the train rushes through the countryside.

### *Cross-curriculum links*

History
Science

## 24: Train journeys

### 1. Night Mail

Listening to and appraising a film soundtrack combining poetry and music.
Composing and arranging music in response to poetry.
Listening to and appraising their own and others' compositions.

**LISTENING PIECE**

*'Night Mail', poem by W. H. Auden (1907–73) music by Benjamin Britten (1913–76) (track 84)*

Auden's poem was written for the documentary film 'Night Mail', made in 1936 by the Post Office Film Unit. The film shows the nightly run of the 'Postal Special' train from London to Scotland, collecting, sorting and delivering mail. The poem is divided into four different sections, the first and third being full of rhythm and rhyming words, which evoke and simulate the relentless sound of the postal train on its important journey. In the second and fourth sections the poet changes this regular rhythm for a more arbitrary, free-flowing mode.

The rhythm of the music that accompanies the poem matches the rhythm of the words, and they combine to create a wonderful sound-picture of the train journey.

The video of 'Night Mail' is available from The Post Office Film and Video Library, PO Box 145, Sittingbourne, Kent, ME10 1NH (Tel: 01795 426465).

### 2. Poor Paddy

*Version 1: Unison (track 85)*
*Version 2: Chorus sung as a round (track 86)*

Singing in two independent parts.
Accompanying a song with improvised ostinato patterns.

**TASK (individuals or groups; *The Purple Book*, p.23)**

This version of the song printed here does not have a verse for 1845.
The children might like to make up a verse themselves.

### 3. Saying your lines

Experimenting with word patterns and integrating them into a composition.
Extending a composition which combines instrumental and vocal ideas.
Performing and appraising their own and others' compositions.

**LISTENING PIECE**

*'Different Trains', Steve Reich (born 1936) (track 87)*

This piece was written in 1988 for string quartet and pre-recorded sound. It uses speech recordings as a stimulus for musical ideas. The composer remembers travelling by train as a child between New York and Los Angeles, with his governess. Although he looks back on his experience as enjoyable, he also realizes that if he had been living at that time in Europe, as a Jew he might have travelled on a very different train. When researching material to create this piece he recorded conversations with his governess and, survivors of the Holocaust, and American and European train sounds of the 1930s and 1940s.

### Cross-curriculum links

Language and poetry
History

# 1: *Exploring sounds*

## Resources

The Pink Book

A range of tuned and untuned percussion instruments, including some which can produce long sounds, e.g. cymbal and metallophone, ideally one instrument per child

## Key vocabulary

Long (**sustained**) sounds

Short (separate) sounds

## Previous experience

Playing a range of tuned and untuned percussion instruments.

Knowing the names of the instruments.

Combining sounds to create simple compositions.

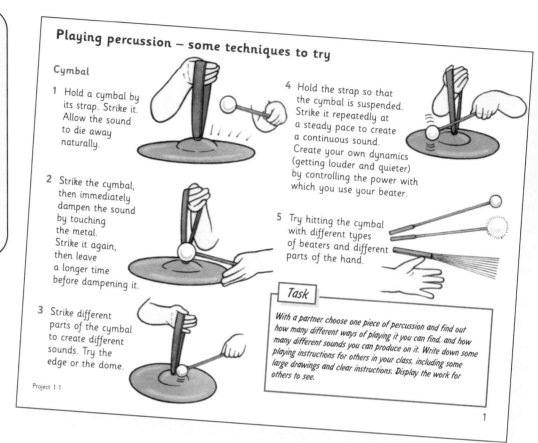

### Playing percussion – some techniques to try

**Cymbal**

1 Hold a cymbal by its strap. Strike it. Allow the sound to die away naturally.

2 Strike the cymbal, then immediately dampen the sound by touching the metal. Strike it again, then leave a longer time before dampening it.

3 Strike different parts of the cymbal to create different sounds. Try the edge or the dome.

4 Hold the strap so that the cymbal is suspended. Strike it repeatedly at a steady pace to create a continuous sound. Create your own dynamics (getting louder and quieter) by controlling the power with which you use your beater.

5 Try hitting the cymbal with different types of beaters and different parts of the hand.

**Task**

With a partner choose one piece of percussion and find out how many different ways of playing it you can find, and how many different sounds you can produce on it. Write down some playing instructions for others in your class, including some large drawings and clear instructions. Display the work for others to see.

Project 1:1

1

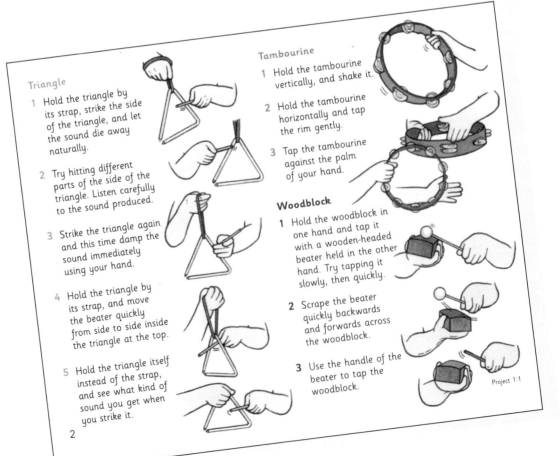

**Triangle**

1 Hold the triangle by its strap, strike the side of the triangle, and let the sound die away naturally.

2 Try hitting different parts of the side of the triangle. Listen carefully to the sound produced.

3 Strike the triangle again and this time damp the sound immediately using your hand.

4 Hold the triangle by its strap, and move the beater quickly from side to side inside the triangle at the top.

5 Hold the triangle itself instead of the strap, and see what kind of sound you get when you strike it.

**Tambourine**

1 Hold the tambourine vertically, and shake it.

2 Hold the tambourine horizontally and tap the rim gently.

3 Tap the tambourine against the palm of your hand.

**Woodblock**

1 Hold the woodblock in one hand and tap it with a wooden-headed beater held in the other hand. Try tapping it slowly, then quickly.

2 Scrape the beater quickly backwards and forwards across the woodblock.

3 Use the handle of the beater to tap the woodblock.

Project 1:1

2

*The Pink Book, pages 1 & 2*

- With the children sitting in a circle, ask them to strike their instruments once, in turn, around the circle.

- Repeat the activity, but this time ask the children to wait until the sound of each instrument has died away before the next one is played.

- Ask the children which instruments produce the longer sounds and which produce the shorter sounds.

- Does what an instrument is made of affect the length of the sound it makes?

- What other factors can affect the length of the sound (*e.g. the way the instrument is struck, held, or suspended)?*

- Ask the children to look at pages 1 and 2 of the Pupils' Book to find more ways to play percussion instruments.

- Ask the children holding the sustaining instruments to find ways of producing short sounds.

- Play round the circle again, with each child making one short sound on their instrument.

- Now ask the children to find ways of making short-sounding instruments produce continuous sounds (*e.g. by scraping a woodblock with the handle of a beater, by sliding (glissando) a beater across the bars of a xylophone, or by using two beaters to play a roll. This last technique needs practice!).*

- Ask the children to try to produce a continuous sound which travels around the circle. (*This can be done by making each sound overlap with the next.*)

Loud and quiet sounds
- Ask the children to vary the dynamics as their individual sounds are passed round the circle. Let them decide how they are going to play their sounds (*e.g. loud or quiet, or gradually growing louder or quieter*).

Long, short, and continuous sounds
- Encourage the children to think of ways of using silence while playing their sounds round the circle (*e.g. try leaving a long silence after a long sound, again after a short sound, and silences of different lengths*).

- Experiment with making many short sounds, to contrast with a long, sustained sound.

- Choose a child to conduct, letting the conductor decide when and how the players should make their sounds. (*The conductor will need to devise three different signals to indicate long, short, and continuous sounds, and a clear 'stop' signal.*)

# 2: Exploring and scoring

**Resources**

The Pink Book

Instruments as for Unit 1

Paper and felt-tip pens

Copy of the blank grid on page 155, for each child

**Key vocabulary**

**Graphic notation**

Grid

**Previous experience**

Using simple notations.

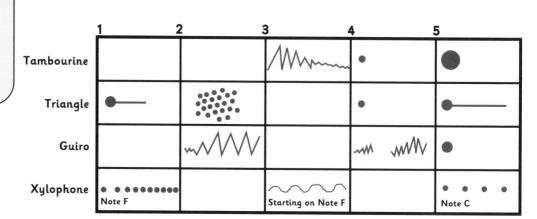

| | 1 | 2 | 3 | 4 | 5 |
|---|---|---|---|---|---|
| Tambourine | | | (jagged line) | • | ⬤ |
| Triangle | •— | (cluster of dots) | | • | •— |
| Guiro | | (zigzag) | | (small zigzag) (zigzag) | ⬤ |
| Xylophone | • • • • • • • • • Note F | | (wavy line) Starting on Note F | | • • • • • Note C |

a short sound played quietly

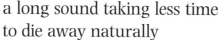

a short sound played medium loud

a short sound played loudly

a long sound dying away naturally

a long sound taking less time
to die away naturally

lots of short sounds played quietly

separate short sounds played slowly

a smooth continuous sound

a continuous sound getting louder

separate sounds getting faster

**A** *discuss*

- Ask the children to recall the sounds they created in the previous lesson *(long, short, continuous)* and how they made them.

- In what different ways can long, short, and continuous sounds be written down? Invite individual children to share their ideas with the class.

- Discuss similar and different ideas, and the reasons for writing specific sounds in particular ways.

- Discuss with the children the different ways that sounds can be notated. Page 3 of the Pupils' Book shows some ways.

- Look at the graphic score on page 3 of the Pupils' Book (and opposite).

- Ask the children to identify the instruments being played *(tambourine, triangle, guiro, xylophone)*.

- Ask more questions to make sure that the children understand how the piece should be performed, e.g.

    Which instruments are playing at box 3? *(Tambourine and xylophone.)*

    Is the triangle playing at box 3? *(No.)*

    How do the players know when to move on to the next box? *(The group might have a conductor or leader, but otherwise the players must listen very carefully and watch the music.)*

- Let four children perform the piece, and ask the rest to comment on their performance.

**B** *compose*

- Distribute the instruments so that each group can make as wide a range of sounds as possible. Give each group a blank grid and some felt-tip pens. *(Paper will be needed for drafting ideas.)*

- Ask the children to compose a piece of music for three or four players which incorporates long, short, and continuous sounds. *(They should use the grid to map out who plays what and when, and they will need to discuss and experiment with ideas before they make final decisions about their pieces, which they should write down in graphic notation.)*

**Keep this work for use in the next unit.**

# 3: Exploring and recording

**Resources**

As for Project 1, Unit 2, plus The Pink Book

Cassette recorder

Blank tape

Children's graphic scores saved from Project 1, Unit 2

**Key vocabulary**

Performance

Interpretation

**Previous experience**

Simple composing tasks.

Classroom performances.

*Yellow-Red-Blue* by Wassily Kandinsky (1866–1944)

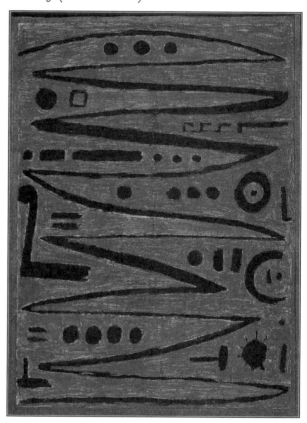

*Heroic Strokes of the Bow*
*by Paul Klee (1879–1940)*

*The Pink Book, pages 4 & 5*

- Give the groups time to complete their graphic scores from Unit 2, and/or practise playing their music. Make sure the names of the instruments are written on the score. (*A spelling checklist may be useful.*)

- Make sure that each group has decided how they will know when to move on to the next box. (*There must be a united group decision about this.*)

- Record the pieces as they are performed. (*Announce the names of the players before each recording.*)

- Analyse the individual compositions with the pupils, considering the overall effect of the pieces.

- What different techniques were used to create the different sounds (*e.g. tapping, scraping, shaking*)?

    How effective was the use of silence?

    Could they hear exactly when the instruments were playing?

    Were all the instruments playing at once, or did the piece use different combinations of a few instruments?

    Did some sounds overlap?

- Encourage the children to try to interpret one another's pieces by swapping music and instruments among the groups.

- Record the performances.

- Make the grids and cassette recordings available so that the children can compare different recordings of the same pieces.

- Ask the children to look on pages 4 and 5 of the Pupils' Book at the paintings *Yellow-Red-Blue* by Wassily Kandinsky, and *Heroic Fiddling* by Paul Klee. (*These are art works which transmit rhythmic movement through shape and form.*)

- Encourage the children to use these pictures as a stimulus for making up their own music.

- Encourage them to translate their own musical ideas into art work.

# 1: Doo-be doo

Traditional tune

**Resources**
The Pink Book

Recording
tracks 1 and 2

**Key vocabulary**
**Pulse**
On the **beat**/off
the beat

**Previous
experience**
Tapping and feeling
the speed of a steady
pulse when singing.

Songs, and listening
to recorded music.

Using vocal and body
sounds.

Doo - wah,  doo - wah,  doo-wah doo - be doo - be doo, oh  yeah.

Doo - wah,  doo - wah,  doo - wah doo - be doo - be  doo.

1. Clap off the beat

Doo - wah,  doo - wah,  doo - wah  doo -be doo - be dooh, oh yeah.  Doo - wah...

2. Clap on the beat

Doo - wah,  doo - wah,  doo - wah  doo - be doo - be dooh, oh  yeah.  Doo - wah...

*The Pink Book, page 6*

 **A**  sing

- Play the song, 'Doo-be doo' (track 1) several times (see page 6 of the Pupils' Book).
- Sing the song with the children, clapping on the beats marked in example 1 above.
- Sing the song again, clapping on the beats marked in example 2 above.
- Ask the children if their clapping changed the feel of the piece. (*The first activity created the feel of an off-the-beat pattern because of the stronger sound on the second and fourth beats. The repeat of the activity created a feel of an on-the-beat pattern because the stronger sound came on the first and third beats.*)

**B** play listen

- Ask each child in turn to clap once around the circle. (*Decide on the speed before you start and try to keep the beat steady.*)
- If this goes well, ask the children to clap one beat, and alternately tap one beat on their knees around the circle.

|  |  |  |  |  |  |
|---|---|---|---|---|---|
| *1* | *2* | *1* | *2* | *1* | *2* |
| *Clap* | *Tap* | *Clap* | *Tap* | *Clap* | *Tap* |

- Try this activity again, this time asking the children to keep their eyes closed. *(Removing the visual element allows the children to listen carefully and concentrate.)*

- Ask the children which of the two sounds feels the stronger.

- Repeat this activity, this time starting with a tap,

|  |  |  |  |  |  |
|---|---|---|---|---|---|
| *1* | *2* | *1* | *2* | *1* | *2* |
| *Tap* | *Clap* | *Tap* | *Clap* | *Tap* | *Clap* |

- Ask the children which beat feels the stronger.

- Extend the activity in different ways by: using a faster pulse; using two different and contrasting body and vocal sounds.

- Listen to the extract from the reggae track recorded by Bob Marley and the Wailers (track 2).

- Ask the children to try to click or tap their fingers on the off-beat.

 **compose**

- In groups, ask each child in turn to create either a body or vocal sound. *(The children should try to create contrasting sounds which will fit into a steady pulse.)*

- Let the group members decide the order in which they want to make their individual sounds, then practise fitting the sounds, one at a time, into a steady pulse.

- Let the children repeat this pattern several times. *(Children working in a group of four will find that their pattern falls into a natural four-beat grouping, whilst the pattern created by a group of three will fall into a three-beat grouping.)*

| *tap* | *clap* | *click* | *stamp* | *tap* | *clap* | *click* | *stamp* |
|---|---|---|---|---|---|---|---|
| *1* | *2* | *3* | *4* | *1* | *2* | *3* | *4* |

| *tap* | *clap* | *stamp* | *tap* | *clap* | *stamp* |
|---|---|---|---|---|---|
| *1* | *2* | *3* | *1* | *2* | *3* |

- Record, on a graphic score, the sound patterns created by each group, to be used in the next lesson.

# 2: *Patterns*

### Resources
The Pink Book

Recording
track 3

Children's
graphic scores
from Project 2,
Unit 1

**Key vocabulary**
**Structure**
**Musical score**

**Previous
experience**
Composing in
small groups.

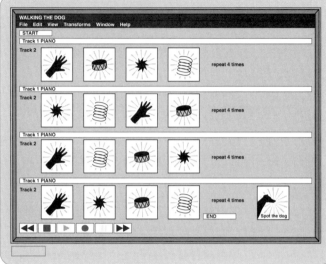

*The Pink Book, page 7*

---

**A**

- Give the groups a short time to practise playing their music from Unit 1, if necessary using the notes they wrote down.

- Invite the groups to perform their patterns.

- Discuss the patterns with the children.

    Has any group created the same, or a similar pattern, to another group?

    Can they hear stronger sounds within the different patterns?

    Has any group chosen to use *either* body *or* vocal sounds?

    Has any group chosen to include both body *and* vocal sounds?

    Did the groups perform their sounds at different speeds?

---

**B**

- Ask the children to choose a pattern created by one of the groups during the last unit.

- Invite the class to perform this pattern, performing the sounds, one at a time, around the circle.

- Repeat this activity, using other patterns invented during Unit 1.

- Ask the children to choose the three or four sounds they created last time and re-arrange them in a new order, e.g.
  *Pattern 1: Clap Click Ooh! Bang! changes to Pattern 2: Click Bang! Ooh! Clap*

  (*The strong sounds are heard on beats 1 and 4 in the first pattern, and on beats 2 and 4 in the second pattern.*)
- Ask the children to try to link the two patterns together to create a longer, eight-beat pattern.

- There are many ways in which they can structure a short piece of music, using the patterns they have invented, e.g.
  *Pattern 1 Pattern 2 Pattern 1 Pattern 2 OR Pattern 1 Pattern 1 Pattern 2 Pattern 2*

- Give the children time to practise their pieces, then invite one group to perform their piece to the class.

- Discuss the piece. Did they hear how the second pattern differs from the first?

  How many times is each pattern played?

  On which beats are the stronger sounds?

  How did the performing group decide how to structure their piece?

- Listen to the other pieces, encouraging the children to talk about what they have heard.

- Encourage the performers to talk about *how* they made their pieces.

- Ask the children to write down their patterns, using an x for the strong beat and o for the weak beat.

- Listen to the recording on track 3. (*Don't let the children look at the Pupils' Book yet.*) If necessary play the recording more than once.

  How many sounds did they hear? (*There are four distinctive sounds played over a piano accompaniment.*)

  Can they describe each sound?

- Play the recording again, and ask them to listen for the changing order of the four sounds.

  How many times is each group of sounds played? (*Four times.*)

  What is the surprise sound at the end? (*A dog barks.*)

- Let the children look at the score of the piece on page 7 of the Pupils' Book while you play the recording again.

# 1: Threes, fours and fives

**Resources**
The Pink Book
Recording tracks 4, 5, and 6

**Key vocabulary**
**Pulse**
**Tempo**
**Time signature**
and beat grouping

**Previous experience**
Keeping a steady beat.

Rhythm patterns from Handel's 'Fireworks' music.

Rhythm from the Prokofiev 'March'.

Rhythm from 'Mars' by Holst.

*These three notes are played in the time of one crochet beat.

*The Pink Book, pages 8 & 9*

**A** play

- Ask one child to act as leader to clap or tap a steady pulse.
- Invite all the children to join in.
- Ask another leader to take over and tap a steady pulse at a different speed.
- With all the children joining in, ask them to notice whether the pulse is at a faster or slower tempo.
- Ask the next leader to accent the first of every four claps. (*This divides the pulse into a four-beat grouping.*)

4 beats

- Ask the children to try these as well:

3 beats

| XOO | XOO | XOO |
|---|---|---|

(three-beat grouping)

5 beats

| XOOOO | XOOOO | XOOOO |
|---|---|---|

(five-beat grouping)

- Ask the first child in the circle to clap the three-beat grouping, the second the four-beat grouping, and the third the five-beat grouping, as follows:

| ₃ Paul | ₄ Sue | ₅ Sonia |
|---|---|---|
| XOO | XOOO | XOOOO |

- Try again with the next three children in the circle, then all the way round the circle, reminding the children to keep a steady beat. *(The children will have to be alert as the patterns should follow on continuously, with no gaps.)*

- Ask the children for ideas about how to decide who will play with which grouping, e.g. according to the colour of their clothes:

| ₄ Blue | Blue | ₃ Red | ₅ Yellow |
|---|---|---|---|
| XOOO | XOOO | XOO | XOOOO |

B   listen

- Ask the children if they can identify the different beat groupings of the three musical extracts on tracks 4, 5, and 6. *(Play each track several times.)*

- Let them look at the information on pages 8 and 9 of the Pupils' Book. *(This shows them the rhythms of the three pieces they have been listening to.)*

C   play

- Invite a child to choose one beat grouping and to clap it, accenting the first beat.

- Ask another child to make up a clapping pattern which will fit into this beat grouping.

- Continue improvising using each of the three-/four-/, and five-beat groupings.

# 2: Transforming the pulse

## Resources

The Pink Book

A range of tuned and untuned percussion instruments

## Key vocabulary

Transform

**Accent**

Steady **beat**

## Previous experience

Keeping a steady beat.

Playing and listening to different pulse groupings.

*The Pink Book, page 10*

---

**A**  *discuss*

- Ask the children to look at the picture on page 10 of the Pupils' Book.

- Ask them what is happening. *(In each picture, the number 4 is fed into the transformer and more numbers are added to it to make the total up to 12.)*

- Ask the children how many more ways they can find for doing this. Choose one of the ways *(e.g. 4+6+2)*, and show the children how it can be clapped by accenting the first beat of each group:

  4 + 6 + 2 = 12

  | **X** 0 0 0 | **X** 0 0 0 0 0 | **X** 0 |
  |---|---|---|
  | 1 2 3 4 | 1 2 3 4 5 6 | 1 2 |

  =12

- Repeat the pattern a number of times, keeping a steady pulse.

**B**   *compose*

- Ask groups of children to make up some 'transformer music' of their own, and to find their own way of writing it down to show that the first beat of each group of beats is stronger, e.g.:

$4 + 3 + 3 + 2 = 12$

| **X**ooo | **X**oo | **X**oo | **X**o | **X**ooo | **X**oo | **X**oo | **X**o |
|---|---|---|---|---|---|---|---|
| 1234 | 123 | 123 | 12 | 1234 | 123 | 123 | 12 |

$4 + 5 + 3 = 12$

| **X**ooo | **X**oooo | **X**oo | **X**ooo | **X**oooo | **X**oo |
|---|---|---|---|---|---|
| 1234 | 12345 | 123 | 1234 | 12345 | 123 |

Allow the children time to practise clapping and tapping their patterns.

- Ask the children to experiment with using two different hand sounds so that the accents can be clearly heard.

- Ask them to try clapping the patterns at different speeds, and then to describe the way in which this changes the feel of the music. *(Make sure that everyone in the group comes in at the same speed – someone may need to count the group in, quietly.)*

*extension activity*    *play*

- Ask the children to play the 'transformer music' on untuned percussion instruments.

- Ask them to combine two different patterns.

- Ask them to make one or two of the beats silent. *(This adds more interest to the music, as replacing sounded beats with rests will effectively change the music from steady pulse to rhythm.)*

| **X** | **X**oo | **X**oo-o | **X**o- |
|---|---|---|---|
| 1 | 123 | 12345 | 123 |

# 1: Hill an' gully

**Resources**

The Pink Book

Recording track 7 ☐

A range of percussion instruments

**Key vocabulary**

**Calypso**

**Call and response**

**Previous experience**

Keeping a steady beat.

Caribbean calypso

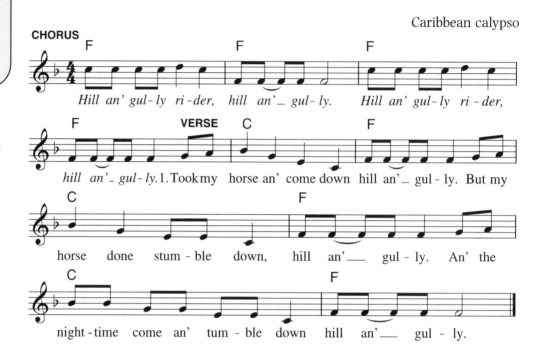

CHORUS

Hill an' gul-ly ri-der, hill an'_ gul-ly. Hill an' gul-ly ri-der,

VERSE

hill an'_ gul-ly. 1. Took my horse an' come down hill an'_ gul-ly. But my

horse done stum-ble down, hill an'___ gul-ly. An' the

night-time come an' tum-ble down hill an'___ gul-ly.

2.      Oh the moon shine bright down, hill an' gully.
       Ain't no place to hide down, hill an' gully.
       An' a zombie come a ridin' down, hill an' gully.
       CHORUS: *Hill an' gully rider* ...

3.      Oh, my knees they shake down, hill an' gully.
       An' my heart starts quakin' down, hill an' gully.
       Ain't nobody goin' to get me down, hill an' gully.
       CHORUS: *Hill an' gully rider* ...

4.      That's the last I set down, hill an' gully.
       Pray the Lord don't let me down, hill an' gully.
       An' I run till daylight breakin' down, hill an' gully.
       CHORUS: *Hill an' gully rider* ...

*The Pink Book, page 11*

This is a calypso from Jamaica, one of the many islands which make up the West Indies. The words are written in Jamaican dialect. The song falls into a 4-beat rhythm and is composed in a call and response style (also known as 'question and answer'). The call is intended to be sung by a solo voice and the response 'hill an' gully' by everyone.

- Ask the children to listen to the recording of the song several times, so that when they are ready they can try clapping or finger-clicking the pulse.

- Ask them to stand up and sway in time to the music, shifting their weight from one foot to the other on the steady beat:

```
Sing   Hill an'    gully    ri - der,    hill an' –  gul – ly————
Clap   x           x        x    x       x      x           x    x
Sway   o                    o            o                  o
```

- Learn the song. *(See page 11 of the Pupils' Book. It is easier if at first everyone sings the whole song.)*

- Invite one child or a small group to sing the 'call' while the rest sing the 'response' *(highlighted in red in the Pupils' Book).*

- Ask the children to listen to the rhythm of the response, then to clap the rhythm as they sing it.

- Ask them how many different notes they would need to play the response. *(One.)*

- Invite one child to play the response rhythm Hill an' gully, playing the F bar on any percussion instrument, and using two beaters alternately.

- Give other children a chance to play.

- Choose two children sitting together, asking the first child to clap the 'Hill an' gully rider' call, whilst the second claps the response:

Rosie (call)                    Ahmed (response)

Hill an' gul-ly ri - der,    hill an'    gul - ly.

- Let other children try this in pairs.

- When this is secure, ask the children to try passing the rhythms round the circle, with alternate children clapping the 'call' and 'response'. (Some children may want to clap the different rhythms of the calls in the other verses.)

# 2: Call and response

**Resources**

The Pink Book

Recording track 7

A range of untuned and tuned percussion instruments

**Key vocabulary**

Accompaniment

**Balance** of sound

**Dynamics**

**Previous experience**

Knowing the song 'Hill an' gully' (Project 4, Unit 1).

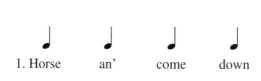

1. Horse      an'      come      down

2. Night - time   come   an'   tum - ble   down

3. Hill   an'   gul - ly   ri - der,   hill   an'___   gul - ly.

*The Pink Book, page 11*

**A**  sing  play

- Revise the song 'Hill an' gully'.

- Ask the children to choose a four-beat rhythm from the song which can be repeated to form an accompaniment, (*e.g. rhythm no.1 or rhythm no. 2, above, see page 11 of the Pupils' Book*).

- Let the children decide how many instruments are needed to balance the singing, and which sounds would be best.

- Help the children to perform the song and accompaniment, taking turns to be singers and players. (Start the players first, then encourage them to listen carefully and keep in time with the singing. If they find it difficult, choose a small group of children to help the players by quietly repeating the words of their rhythm.)

If the singing and playing are going well, try the following:
- Ask the children to use a longer rhythm *(e.g. no. 3)* for the accompaniment opposite.

- Ask them to use two rhythms at once *(e.g. a woodblock for rhythm no. 1, a drum for rhythm no. 2).*

- Ask the children to invent their own call rhythms. *(Each child in turn claps a call rhythm, with everybody clapping the 'Hill an' gully' response after each call. Some children might clap one of the rhythms from the song, whilst others might feel confident enough to invent their own. If some children encounter difficulty, encourage them to say their chosen words while they clap, and/or invite one of them to play the four-beat pulse on a drum, as a supportive framework.)*

- If this activity goes well, invite the children to make up a response of their own to replace 'Hill an' gully'.

- Ask groups of children to compose a piece of music which has a call and response structure. *(They should decide on a rhythm for the response and practise playing all together and in time with each other.)*

- Next, they should choose one member of the group to play a steady beat, while the others each create a different call rhythm.

- Finally, ask them to decide on the best order for the call rhythms.

- Let each group play their piece to the others.

- Ask the children to think of ways in which they could use contrasting dynamics in their pieces, and in the song *(e.g. a loud call may be answered by a quiet response, or vice versa).*

# 3: Echo song

**Resources**

The Pink Book

Recording tracks 8 and 9

Tambour, tambourine, triangle, and cymbal

Some tuned percussion instruments

**Key vocabulary**

Imitation

**Sustain**

Two-part

**Previous experience**

Investigating and playing percussion instruments (see Project 1).

Music and words: Jan Holdstock

*The Pink Book, page 12*

- Let the children listen to version 1 of the song *(track 8)*, then practise joining in with the echo, taking plenty of breath to help with sustaining the long notes.

- Divide the class into two and sing both parts, the second part as an echo *(more quietly and distant-sounding)*.

- Look at page 12 of the Pupils' Book, let them see how the two parts are written out.

- Ask them which word had the longest note. *(Echo has eight beats in all.)*

### B play

- Listen to version 2 of the song on track 9. *(This is performed on a drum and tambourine – no melody.)*

- Ask the children what they can hear *(e.g. how did each instrument sustain the long sound?).*

- Ask two children to sit opposite each other, one with a tambour, the other with a tambourine.

- Invite a third child to tap a steady beat. (This will help the players to keep in time.)

- Ask the tambour player to choose one of the 'Echo song' rhythms, e.g.:

deep      in      the      well,_____

- Let the tambour player start playing her or his chosen rhythm.

- Ask the tambourine player to join in and imitate the tambour rhythm. Pass the instruments on and repeat the activity a few times.

- Pass the instruments on again, but this time ask each player to try to find a way of sustaining their last sound for an extra four beats before starting the rhythm again, while the other player plays.

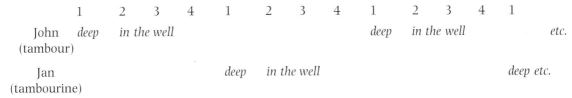

| | 1 | 2 | 3 | 4 | 1 | 2 | 3 | 4 | 1 | 2 | 3 | 4 | 1 | |
|---|---|---|---|---|---|---|---|---|---|---|---|---|---|---|
| John (tambour) | *deep* | *in the well* | | | | | | | *deep* | *in the well* | | | | *etc.* |
| Jan (tambourine) | | | | | *deep* | *in the well* | | | | | | | *deep etc.* | |

- Give out a triangle and a cymbal *(each of which can sustain the sound after being struck).* Work on the overlapping ideas with these two instruments. *(Make sure every child has had a turn with the instruments.)*

### extension activity  compose

- Give the children opportunities to work in pairs on the overlapping ideas.

- Encourage them to make up their own four-beat patterns, reminding them that imitating the rhythms quietly will give their music an echo effect.

- Let the children play their pieces of music.

# 1: The big machine

**Resources**

The Pink Book

Recording track 10

A range of untuned percussion instruments

**Key vocabulary**
**Rhythm pattern**

**Previous experience**

Singing.

Keeping a steady beat.

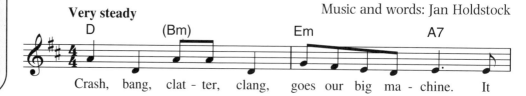

Very steady

Music and words: Jan Holdstock

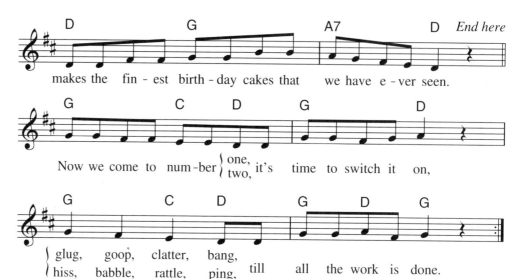

Crash, bang, clat - ter, clang, goes our big ma - chine. It makes the fin - est birth - day cakes that we have e - ver seen.

Now we come to num - ber one, / two, it's time to switch it on,

glug, goop, clatter, bang, / hiss, babble, rattle, ping, till all the work is done.

*There is a piano accompaniment for this song on page 148.*

*The Pink Book, page 13*

**A**   *sing*

- Play the song twice, asking the children to listen for sound words, e.g. rattle, ping.

- Ask the children what noises number 1 machine makes. *(Glug, goop, clatter, bang.)*

- What noises does number 2 machine make? *(Hiss, babble, rattle, ping.)*

- Play the song again, asking the children to look at page 13 of the Pupils' Book to see what the machine makes. *(Birthday cakes.)*

- Think of some more things the machine might make, with the same rhythm pattern as 'birthday cakes' *(e.g. denim jeans, roller-skates, blue ice-cream).*

- Learn and sing 'The big machine'.

**B**  *compose*

- Discuss with the class ideas for inventing their own big machine, made up of several parts, a group to each part.

  What do they want the machine to make?

  What sound words might it use?

- Give each group a number which corresponds to one part of the machine, and make up a short piece for it. *(The children can speak their words, or sing them to the melody of the song. They may wish to exaggerate their words by making them high or low, loud or quiet, but they must keep in time.)*

- Sing through the song, replacing the words 'birthday cake' with whatever they have decided the machine will make, and ask group 1 to perform their words immediately after 'it's time to switch it on'.

- Repeat this activity for each group, singing the appropriate number for each group in the fifth bar (see opposite).

**C**  *sing*

- Ask one of the groups to sing or say their four sound words, keeping a steady beat *(e.g. bang, rattle, pop, crash).*

- Ask another group to join in with their words *(e.g. gurgle, hiss, clank, plip).*

- Invite more groups to join in, without losing the beat. *(If the children can do this well, let them add an instrument to match one of the sound words in each group.)*

*extension activity*  *sing*

- Ask the children to sing the song, starting with the words, 'Now we've got the whole machine, it's time to switch it on'.

- Add in each group, one after the other, finally adding the instruments.

# 2: Central heating

**Resources**
The Pink Book
Paper and
felt-tip pens

**Key vocabulary**
Onomatopoeia
Syllable

**Previous experience**
Experimenting with
the voice to make a
range of sounds.
Using graphic
notation.

There's a Monster in our house,
Our friend the central heating.
From the way its stomach rumbles
Goodness knows what it's been eating!

It wakes us up at night-time
With its gurglings and its groanings,
Its clatterings and its clangings,
Its mutterings and moanings.

Mum says it lives on water,
In answer to my question.
I think that it must gulp it down
To get such indigestion!

*John Foster*

*The Pink Book, page 14*

*This poem conveys wonderfully the sound made by a central heating system. Its language is vivid and evocative, particularly in the use of alliteration and onomatopoeia in the second verse.*

**A**  *discuss*

- Read the poem with the children (page 14 of the Pupils' Book).

- Ask the children which words describe the noises the central heating makes. *(Read the poem again so that the children can listen for those words.)*

- Ask the children to discover ways in which words like 'mutterings and moanings' can be imaginatively sounded to express the range of sounds the central heating system can make *(e.g. try lengthening or shortening the syllables)*.

- What other kinds of machines are found in the home or belong to the family? *(e.g. motorbike, hair dryer, electric drill, washing machine.)*

**B**    *sing*

- Ask the children to think of words for the sounds which are made by a washing machine.

- Ask them to link some words which start with the same letters *(e.g. swishing and swashing, splishing and sploshing, whirring and whizzing, burring and buzzing, clicking and clunking).*

- Share the ideas and write them down so that everyone can see them.

**C**    *discuss*

- Ask the children to help you to write out, on a large piece of paper, a programme for a washing machine. *(They can use the picture on page 15 of the Pupils' Book to help them.)*

- Discuss and try out ways in which sounds could be used to imitate these processes. *(Some sounds will keep to a pulse, others will not.)*

- In groups, ask the children to use invented words and syllables, as well as descriptive words, to imitate the sounds of the machine.

- Share the different ideas, and notice that some sections are more rhythmic than others.

- Are there any sounds which could be improved by saying them in a different way? *(e.g. exaggerating certain syllables – swishshshshing.)*

**D**    *discuss*

- Explore ways of drawing the words and sounds that they have already made up. *(Page 15 of the Pupils' Book will give them some ideas.)*

- Ask the children to explore the ideas shared in the class sessions, and their ideas, using only their voices. *(They must listen carefully, and write down the words so that they look like the actual sound produced.)*

**Save the children's work for Project 5, Unit 3.**

# 3: Machine sounds

**Resources**

The Pink Book

Recording tracks 11 and 12

Paper

A range of coloured felt-tip pens or pencils

Washing machine programme from Project 5, Unit 2

Children's work from Project 5, Unit 2

**Key vocabulary**

**Pitch** direction

high,

low

low ⟶ high

high ⟶ low

**Graphic score**

**Previous experience**

Exploring ideas using the voice.

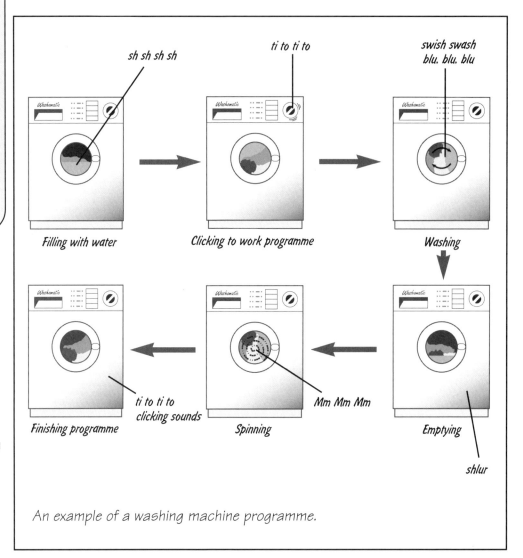

*An example of a washing machine programme.*

   **A**  sing  discuss

*Display the washing machine programme made last lesson.*

• Ask each group to perform the words and sounds they practised in the last lesson, showing how they were written down.

• Decide where the words will fit into the washing machine programme.

**B**   compose listen

- Ask the groups to make up a washing machine piece, using the words and sounds they have practised. *(They may wish to make up more words, or change the way they say them. They will need to decide the order in which the different sounds are to be made. The washing machine programme made in the last session will help with this.)*

- Ask the children to decide whether they want to perform different sounds at the same time, overlap some of the sounds, or use different dynamics and pitches.

- Give the children time to practise and refine their pieces, then record their performances and display their scores.

- Discuss the results with them.

    How were the pieces different?

    Were there any similarities?

    Did the way the words were written match the way they were performed?

    Did the performers use their voices imaginatively?

    Did they perform their compositions with confidence?

*The two recorded extracts, one orchestral, one vocal, have been inspired by machines.*

1  The typewriter *(track 11)*.

- Ask the children if they can hear the sound of the keys being tapped, and the bell that marks the carriage return *(see page 16 in the Pupils' Book)*.

2  Timepiece *(track 12)*.

- Ask the children to listen to the way the singers say 'tick tock' and the 'ticking and the tocking', crisply and in time. Let them look at the pictures of different timepieces on page 16 of the Pupils' Book.

extension activity   compose

- Let the children draw a fantastic machine using some of the ideas from Units 2 and 3 and use it as a graphic score for a composition.

# 1: Monkey chant

**Resources**

The Pink Book

Recording
track 13

**Key vocabulary**

**Accent**

Repetition

**Previous experience**

Being able to keep a steady beat.

An awareness of dynamics.

Combining independent rhythmic ideas.

**Grid A**

| | 1 | 2 | 3 | 4 | 5 | 6 | 7 | 8 |
|---|---|---|---|---|---|---|---|---|
| **1** | 1 | 2 | 3 | 4 | 5 | 6 | 7 | 8 |
| **2** | chat —— ter > | | chat —— ter > | | chat —— ter > | | chat —— ter > | |
| **3** | chat > | | chat > | | chat > | | chat > | |

**Grid B**

| | 1 | 2 | 3 | 4 | 5 | 6 | 7 | 8 |
|---|---|---|---|---|---|---|---|---|
| **4** | | chak > | | chak > | | chak > | | chak > |
| **5** | ke —— chak > | | ke —— chak > | | ke —— chak > | | ke —— chak > | |
| **6** | chakke > | chak | chakke > | chak | chakke > | chak | chakke > | chak |
| **7** | | chakke > | | chakke > | | chakke > | | chakke > |

*The Pink Book, page 18*

**A**   *listen*

- Read to the children the extract from the *Ramayana* story on page 17 of the Pupils' Book.

- Play the recording of 'Monkey chant' to the children, explaining that it accompanies the *Ramayana* story. Invite them to tap in time to the music.

- Ask them to describe what they heard.

  How did the chant convey the sound of chattering monkeys?

- Play the piece again, and ask the children to comment on the speed of the music.

- Ask them to count the number of beats in the repeated melody. *(Eight.)*

**B** *play*

- Tap a steady pulse, and ask the children to count at the same speed from 1 to 8 a number of times.

- Divide the class into three groups, to perform Grid A.

- Ask Group 1 to count from 1 to 8 as before, while Group 2 and 3 chant 'chat-ter, chat-ter', keeping strictly in time with the counting (see score opposite), and remembering the accent on 'chat-'.

- Ask Group 1 to count again, whilst Group 3 chants 'chat' on numbers 1, 3, 5, and 7.

- If this goes well let the children try putting the two lines of the chant together, with Group 1 still counting to keep the beat.

- Let the groups change over so that every group has a go at counting, and at the two different chants.

*extension activity* *play*

- Using the score of 'Monkey chant' in the Pupils' Book (page 18), let the children learn more lines from the chant (Grid B), and ask the children to try performing them all at once, reinforcing the accented syllables. *(A steady beat is needed throughout this piece in order to keep everyone together.)*

- Instead of counting 1 to 8, ask the children to use a sound which is very different from those in the piece *(e.g. a high-pitched voice sounding 'ping' on the beat will permeate the texture)*.

- Practise the chant, changing the parts round, so that each group can perform each rhythmic pattern.

# 2: Gamelan

**Resources**

The Pink Book

Recording track 14

Metallophone, glockenspiels, and chime bars

**Key vocabulary**

Contrast

Indonesia

**Gamelan**

**Previous experience**

Knowing 'Monkey chant' from Project 6, Unit 1.

Simple melodies on tuned percussion.

**Numbered chime bars for 'Monkey chant' melody**

| Numbers for 'Monkey chant' melody |
|---|
| 5   2   5   3   1   3   2   1 |

- Arrange the children so that they are sitting in a circle.
- Using chime bars or a tuned percussion instrument, isolate the four notes of the scale, numbered as shown above and on page 18 of the Pupils' Book.
- Ask the children to sing and memorize the numbers as you play the melody of the numbered notation: 5   2   5   3   1   3   2   1
- Repeat until the children are familiar with the tune and numbers.
- Perform 'Monkey chant', with the melody as an accompaniment performed by a few singers and tuned percussion.

**B** *compose*

- In groups, ask the children to compose their own eight-note tune on the four chime bars.

- Ask them to write down the notes of the melody, using numbers.

- Invite each child in the group to try to play their melody, practising until the melodies are secure.

- Ask one child in the group to play the melody while the others sing the numbers.

**C** *play*

- Ask the children to decide how to perform 'Monkey chant' on page 18 of the Pupils' Book to include contrasting loud and quiet passages (*e.g. four times loudly, then four times quietly, then four times loudly again*).

- Practise the chant, using as many lines as the children can manage.

- Experiment to decide whether the counting group can be left out, cut down, or replaced by one of the group melodies.

**D** *listen*

- Play the Javanese gamelan extract, track 14.

- Ask the children if they can hear what the instruments are made of. (*They are all metal, except the drum.*)

- Let them look at the instruments in the photograph on page 19 of the Pupils' Book.

- Does the music stay at the same speed throughout the piece? (*It speeds up, then slows down at the end.*)

*extension activity* *play*

- Let the children dramatize the *Ramayana* story from Unit 1 of this project, about the rescue of Princess Sita by the monkey army (*see the story on page 17 of the Pupils' Book*).

- Include a performance of 'Monkey chant'.

- Use some of the melodies the children have composed to accompany the drama.

# 1: Droning on

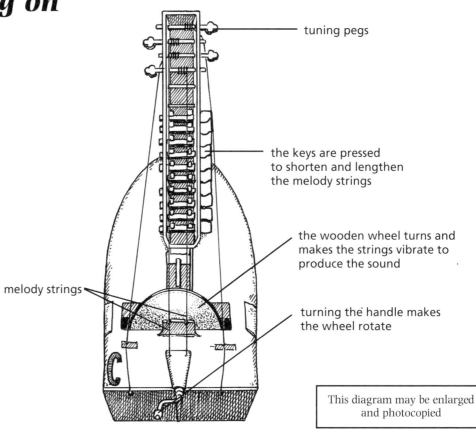

tuning pegs

the keys are pressed
to shorten and lengthen
the melody strings

the wooden wheel turns and
makes the strings vibrate to
produce the sound

melody strings

turning the handle makes
the wheel rotate

> This diagram may be enlarged
> and photocopied

**Resources**

The Pink Book

Recording tracks
15, 16, 17, and 18

A range of tuned
percussion
instruments

Keyboard

Recorder

or guitar
(if available)

**Key vocabulary**
**Drone**
Bagpipe
Tambura
Hurdy-gurdy
Didjeridu
**Sustained**/short

**Previous
experience**
Playing tuned
percussion
instruments.

Simple rhythm work.

The drone is a very ancient musical device used to accompany instrumental
or sung melody. The drone can either be played as a steady stream of sound,
(e.g. bagpipes), or as a repeated sound on the 1st, and sometimes the 5th,
note of the scale (e.g. Indian tambura).

**A**    listen

- Ask the children to listen to the following extracts:

  Indian tambura (track 15)       Irish bagpipe (track 17)
  Australian didjeridu (track 16)    French hurdy-gurdy (track 18)

- Look at pages 20 and 21 of the Pupils' Book and discuss the different instruments.
  Can the children tell what the instruments are made of?
  Can they suggest how each of the instruments is played?

  Can they find out what techniques the players use to create the drone effect?

  Which drones make a continuous sound and which are made up
  of separate sounds? *(The tambura drone is made up of separate sounds.)*

  Which of the instruments can play a drone *and* a melody together?
  *(The bagpipe and the hurdy-gurdy.)*

- Help the children to try to place the instruments in their historical and
  geographical contexts.

*Drones are pitched to the keynote (the first note of a scale), and often to the fifth note above. The distance between two pitches is known as an interval. From G to D is a five-note interval (a 5th):*

Five notes from the scale of G

| G | A | B | C | D |
|---|---|---|---|---|
| 1 | 2 | 3 | 4 | 5 |

- Using the two notes G and D, invite one child to play the two sounds together. *(Two beaters will be needed.)*

- Give other children the opportunity to create a drone effect, by sounding the notes only when the previous sound has died away *(glockenspiel or metallophone)*, and by repeating the notes one after the other, or together *(xylophone)*.

- Ask a child to find a sustained sound. *(If available, use the organ sound on an electric keyboard, or a recorder.)*

- Ask two other children to use recorders, each playing one of the two notes G and D. *(The players should breathe at different times to make the sound continuous.)*

**extension activity**

- Let the children make drones on other instruments, e.g.:
    The four strings of the violin are tuned G (lowest)-D-A-E (highest). If the two bottom strings (G and D) are bowed together they will create a drone.

    The six-stringed guitar is tuned E (lowest)-A-D-G-B-E (highest). The strings D and G can be played alternately or together to form a drone.

    Kazoos can be used to make an effective drone. The sound is resonant, similar to that of the bagpipe, and the children need to create their note for the drone by singing into the instrument.

- Ask the children to play drones on different combinations of instruments simultaneously.

- Ask them to consider balance of sound. *(They must listen carefully and make sure the drones blend together.)*

- Ask them to create some simple rhythmic patterns for the drones.

- Ask the children which combinations of instruments they think sound well together.

# 2: *Round and round*

**Resources**

The Pink Book

Recording tracks
19 and 20

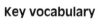

Tuned percussion
instruments –
xylophone,
metallophone,
glockenspiel

Electronic
keyboard

Any other
instruments which
can play the drone
notes D and A,
e.g. violin, guitar,
cello

**Key vocabulary**

Accompaniment

Verse and chorus

**Coda**

**Previous experience**

Creating and
playing a simple
accompaniment
to a song.

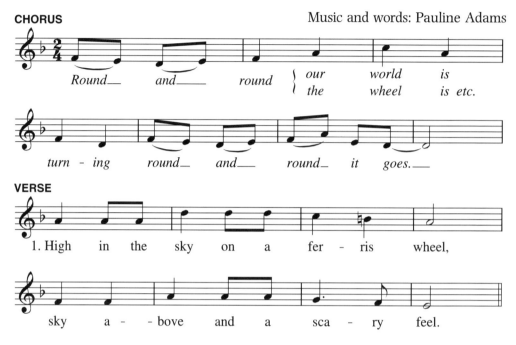

Music and words: Pauline Adams

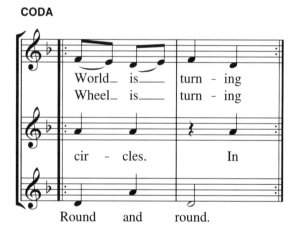

*Round and round our world is turning,*
*round and round it goes.*

2. Circling around on the ferris wheel,
   sky above and a scary feel.

*Round and round the wheel is turning,*
*round and round it goes.*

3. Kite flying free on a clear cold day,
   sun and warmth so far away.

*Round and round the fields are turning,*
*round and round they go.*

4. Over the sea a seabird wheels,
   wind is fresh, how good it feels.

*Round and round the air is turning,*
*round and round it goes.*

5. Speeding in space to the dusty moon,
   earth below, hope to get back soon.

*Round and round our world is turning,*
*round and round it goes.*

*The Pink Book, page 22*

**A  sing  play**

- Play the children the first recording of the song.

- Ask them if the song is sung with or without an accompaniment. *(It is with accompaniment.)*

- Ask them to describe the accompaniment. *(The song is accompanied by a drone.)*

- Listen to the recording of the song again, and join in the chorus. *(Each chorus is slightly different, as first the world turns, then the wheel, fields, air, and finally in the last chorus, the world again.)*

- When the children are confident about singing the chorus, learn each verse. *(The words are on page 22 of the Pupils' Book.)*

- Choose some instruments to play the drone on notes D and A.

- Remind the children of the different combinations and ways they have already tried *(Unit 1)*.

- Ask them to think of different ways of playing the drone. *(For example, try using pitched instruments in different combinations, to accompany the verse.)*

- Ask the children if they can think of any other ways to accompany the song.

**extension activity  sing**

- Listen to the second version of 'Round and round' (track 20).

- Ask the children how it is different from the first version. *(There is an added section, known as a coda, at the end of the song, which combines three short melodic phrases, each entering at a different time.)*

- Learn to sing the 'Round and round' phrase from the coda, shown on page 22 of the Pupils' Book.

- Ask the children if they have realized that it uses the two pitches of the drone.

- When they are confident in singing the 'Round and round' phrase, add the 'In circles' phrase from the coda.

- Ask the children to listen carefully to the recording so that they know how to fit the two phrases together.

- Sing the two melodies together, then when this is secure add the third part, 'Wheel is turning'.

- Sing the whole song with drone accompaniment, and with the coda, also accompanied by the drone.

- Let the children decide how to finish the song *(e.g. using repetition, fading out, slowing down)*.

# 3: Bach and Bartók

**Resources**

The Pink Book

Recording tracks 21 and 22

A range of tuned percussion instruments

Keyboards

Recorders

**Key vocabulary**

**Scale**

**Improvisation**

**Previous experience**

Simple improvisation.

'Gavotte' by J. S. Bach

'Bagpipe Music' by Bartók

*The Pink Book, pages 23 & 34*

 A **play**

- In the centre of the circle place either chime bars or one tuned percussion instrument with the notes D and A. *(This is to play the drone.)*

- Invite a child to play a repeated short rhythmic drone using a name or word pattern. *(The children can choose one of the patterns from the song they learned in Unit 2, or create their own)* e.g.

  | *1* | *2* | *3* | *4* | | *1* | *2* | *3* | *4* | |
  |---|---|---|---|---|---|---|---|---|---|
  | *Play* | *the* | *drone———* | | , | *Play* | *the* | *drone———* | | , *etc.* |

- Set out another percussion instrument with the following scale, starting on D.

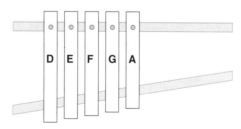

- Invite another child to improvise freely over the drone pattern, using the scale of D.

- Repeat this activity with different children, encouraging them to experiment and be adventurous with their improvisations, but always to listen to, and keep in time with, the pattern of the drone.

*If you have only a few tuned percussion instruments, you will need to introduce this task as a class activity and then, if possible, allow time during the week for small groups to work on their musical ideas. Each group will need two tuned percussion instruments, one for the drone, the other for improvising. Keyboards can be shared.*

- Allow the children to look at the notes of the two differently pitched drones.

**Drone 1**                                                     **Drone 2**

- Ask them to experiment with improvising over each drone, using the same D scale they used in Activity A.

- Then ask them to decide on the drone notes that they like the best, and then let them work on their improvisations using that drone.

- Invite the children to share their improvised music.

- Listen to the two excerpts on tracks 21 and 22.

- Ask the children if they can hear how many instruments are playing on each track? *(One.)*

- What kind of instruments are they, and how are they played? *(Both are keyboards, both composers have tried to create a bagpipe effect in their music.)*

- Ask the children if anyone knows the names of the instruments. *(Bach's music is played by a harpsichord, Bartók's by a piano, see Pupils' Book pages 23 and 24.)*

- Look at the musical extracts *(see opposite and Pupils' Book pages 23 and 24).*

- In Bach's music, ask the children what they notice about the bottom line of the left-hand music. *(It is a one-note drone.)*

- Can the children see the difference between this and the left-hand notes in Bartók's music? *(Bartók's left hand uses two notes – a two-note drone.)*

- Play the music again, asking the children how the composers have succeeded in creating effective drones.

# 1: Ring out!

**Resources**

The Green Book

Recording
track 23 and 24

A range of tuned percussion instruments, keyboards and hand chimes if available

**Key vocabulary**

**Unison**

**Round**

**Chord**

**Previous experience**

Using tuned percussion instruments and keyboards.

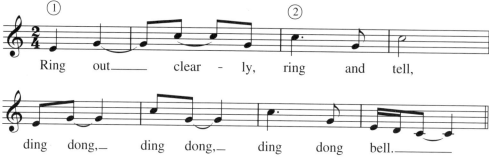

Ring out___ clear - ly, ring and tell,

ding dong,— ding dong,— ding dong bell.___

*The Green Book, page 1*

  **A** *discuss sing*

- Play the unison version of the song (track 23). *(This is based around the chord of C.)*

- Teach the children the whole melody, encouraging them to keep the singing light, but attacking the words 'ding' and 'dong' with a definite 'd' sound.

- When they can do this securely, listen to the second version of the recording (track 24), sung as a round.

- Ask the children if they can hear how the parts fit together *(e.g. when does the second part enter?).*

- Practise singing the song as a round. *(The starting note is E, the second part enters at 2.)*

 **B** *sing play*

- Introduce the children to the chord of C by playing C, E, and G in turn on a metal tuned percussion instrument *(see opposite page).*

- Repeat the three notes, asking the children to sing the letter name of each as it is played.

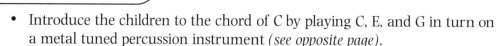

- Invite one child to play the same notes in a different order, while another child turns his or her back to the instrument. Invite the listener to state the order in which the notes are being played.

- Repeat this activity with different children, asking each player to try and think of a different note order.

C  discuss play

- Ask the children to look at, and describe, a keyboard. *(There is a diagram on page 1 of the Pupils' Book. Make sure they notice that it is made up of white and black keys.)*

- Ask them what they notice about the grouping of the white and black keys. *(The black keys are grouped alternately in twos and threes.)*

- If you have a keyboard, can any child identify the C notes? *(C is the white key that comes to the left of each group of two black keys.)*

- If you have an electronic keyboard, invite a child to select a suitable bell sound from the sound bank. *(Or you could use a glockenspiel.)*

- Ask another child to find and play all the Cs.

- Show the children the notes of the chord of C on the keyboard or look at page 2 of the Pupils' Book.

**The notes of the chord of C**

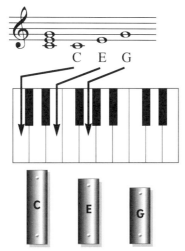

- Invite a child to play the chord of C, sounding C with the thumb, E with the middle finger, and G with the little finger, playing the notes separately or together. *(This will help the children to see and feel the shape of the chord.)*

- Ask the children how many C chords can be made on the keyboard.

# 2: *Tuneful chords*

**Resources**

The Green Book

Recording track 25

A range of tuned percussion instruments, and keyboards and/or chime bars C E G

**Examples of rhythmic patterns**

ring    out_____        ring    and    tell

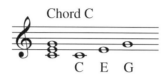

Chord C

C  E  G

**Key vocabulary**

**Chord**

**Ostinato**

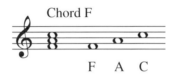

Chord F

F  A  C

**Previous experience**

Playing tuned percussion instruments, using two beaters.

Playing melodic and rhythmic patterns.

Know 'Ring out!', Project 8, Unit 1.

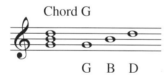

Chord G

G  B  D

- Revise and sing 'Ring out!' from Unit 1, in unison and as a round, with the whole class.

- In groups, ask the children to work out, on their instruments, some of the rhythmic patterns in the round. *(Remind them that the starting note of the round is E, and that quietly singing the melody of the round will help them to work out the different patterns. If they need help, suggest groups of words which create patterns (see above).)*

- When they have done this, ask some groups to repeat their patterns several times, as ostinatos.

- Ask them to try playing the patterns together, repeating them three times.

- Are they happy with the way their patterns sound and fit together?

- Sing 'Ring out!', using the groups' patterns as accompaniments.

**B** *compose*

- Let them look at the chord of C on page 1 of the Pupils' Book (and opposite).

- Ask each group of children to experiment with tunes based on the notes of the chord of C, organizing their ideas into a C chord composition. *(They can use the notes in any order they like, repeat notes and make up rhythm patterns to create added interest.)*

*(This is an example of part of a composition using a steady beat and repeated notes.)*

*(This is an example of part of a composition using rhythm.)*

- Encourage them to experiment with using block chords in their compositions. *(On tuned percussion instruments it is impossible to play the three notes of the chord of C major all at once with only two beaters, but interesting effects can be produced by playing a combination of two notes at once. Those using keyboards will be able to include the three-note block chord by playing all three notes simultaneously.)*

Tunes including chords with two notes together. *(Ways of using two notes of the chord.)*

- Encourage the children to add interest to their pieces by varying dynamics, by introducing some silences (rests), by not all playing all the time, or by having some solo playing.

- Perform and record the compositions.

**C**   *listen* *discuss*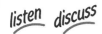

- Look at the picture on page 2 of the Pupils' Book, and play the bugle call (track 25). *(This is based around the notes of one chord. The call uses only these three notes of the chord).*

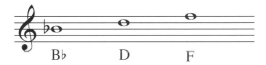

- Introduce the children to some different chords, such as F and G on page 2 of the Pupils' Book (and opposite). Give them time to experiment with these. (They may discover that they can change from one chord to another.)

# 1: Oats and beans

**Resources**

The Green Book

Recording tracks
26, 27, and 28

Tuned percussion
instruments and
keyboards

**Key vocabulary**

**Scale**

**Octave**

Ascending and
descending

**Steps and leaps**

**Sequence**

**Previous
experience**

Familiarity with
using tuned
percussion
and keyboards.

**Oats and beans**

Traditional British song
Words adapted by Pauline Adams

1. Oats and beans and bar-ley grow, oats and beans and bar-ley grow, do

you or I or a-ny-one know how oats and beans and bar-ley grow?

2. **First the farmer sows the seeds,
   then rain and sun provide their needs.
   O stamp your feet and clap your hands,
   and turn around to view the land.**

3. **Gather in the harvest yield
   from the soil within the field.
   The food that's plentiful and there
   for all to eat and all to share.**

*The Green Book, page 3*

**A** sing discuss play

- Learn the whole song (track 26).
- Ask the children to tap the steady beat as they sing.
- Discuss the structure of the song.
- Is there any repetition? *(The first phrase is repeated.)*
- What happens in the second half of the song? *(It moves stepwise down the scale (descending), starting on C and ending on C eight notes (an octave) lower.)*
- Ask the children to raise their hands in the air and move them downwards as they sing the words 'Do you or I. . . ?'

- Invite one child to play down the scale of C, preferably on an alto xylophone or glockenspiel. *(These have notes within the pitch range of the song. Otherwise use any other tuned percussion instrument.)*

- Sing 'Oats and beans' again, this time accompanying the second half of the song from 'Do you' on the xylophone, playing the notes below going down the scale (see opposite), to fit the words 'you or I . . . barley grow':

| C | C | B | B | A | A | A | G | G | F | F | E | E | D | D | C |
|---|---|---|---|---|---|---|---|---|---|---|---|---|---|---|---|
| you | or | I | or | a-ny-one | know | how | oats | and | beans | and | bar-ley | grow? | | | |

*The children can see, on the second line of the song on page 3 of the Pupils' Book, how each of the notes is repeated to fit the rhythm of the words.*

- Listen to version 2 of the song on track 27.

- Ask the children what is different. *(The scale moves upwards – ascending.)*

- Practise the line, 'Do you or I', singing 'Do' on G, then up the scale starting on the low C, using the alto xylophone to pitch the note.

do  you  or  I  or  a-ny-one know how  oats  and beans and bar-ley grow?

- Divide the class into two halves and sing the ascending and descending scales simultaneously. *(All the children start on 'Do', which is pitched on the note G. Make sure each half is secure with their version before they sing together.)*

- Now sing the descending scale as a round (again starting on the word 'Do' at 1), with the second part starting at 2. *(You can hear this on track 28.)*

- Sing all three verses of the song unaccompanied. *(Each verse could be sung in a different version.)*

---

**B**  *compose*

*Each group will need a tuned percussion instrument or a keyboard.*
- Ask the children to explore different ways of playing the notes of the scale of C, ascending and descending.

e.g.: leaping over notes

C'  A  F  C,

using sequences

C  C  E  D  D  F  E  E  G  F  F  A  and so on . . .

- Play and discuss the different and similar ideas.

# *2: Raga moods*

### Resources

The Green Book

Recording track 29

Keyboards and recorders, and percussion instruments, preferably chromatic, which can sustain sound – metallophones, glockenspiels, and metal chime bars

### Key vocabulary

**Raga**

Mood

**Alap**

**Sustained** sounds

### Previous experience

Exploring and playing scales.

Playing long and short sounds.

Awareness of pitch direction.

*The Green Book, page 3*

**A** play listen

- With the children sitting in a circle, place two metallophones or glockenspiels in the middle of the circle. Take off all the bars except the following: C, D, E, G, B on one instrument, and C, D, F♯, G, B, C on the other.

- Invite a child to choose one of the scale patterns from page 3 of the Pupils' Book, and below, and then to start playing at the bottom of the scale, on the lowest note, slowly moving towards the highest note.

C D E G B

C D F♯ G B C

- Ask the child to let some of the notes die away naturally before playing the next note.

- Listen on track 29 to the way the Indian flute player combines longer and shorter sounds as he unfolds a pentatonic raga called 'Jait'. He plays the notes of the scale before he begins his improvisation.

- Listen to the way the music weaves around the notes of the scale – there are no sudden jumps or leaps.

**B**  compose discuss

- In groups, ask the children to invent their own scale or note row (*of not more than seven notes within one octave*), using tuned percussion, keyboards or recorders.
  (*They will find the following a helpful guide when constructing their scales:*

  - *the scale can start on any note, and include sharps and flats (the black notes on a keyboard)*
  - *within one octave they can choose any notes from the 12 pitches available.*)

C   Db   E   F   *Ab   B   C

\* Same note as G♯.

*An example of a six-note scale*

- Encourage the children to try out a number of different scale patterns before deciding on one they particularly like and want to use for creating their own music.

- Encourage the children to create their own music in the style of an alap (*see glossary, page 158*) by exploring different ways of gradually moving up their chosen scale, then down again, step by step. Remind them to make some notes longer than others and to explore the scale by weaving around adjacent notes as they move upwards and then downwards, back to where they began.

- Keyboard players may find using a sustained 'voice' more effective.

- Ask each group to perform their alap, but first ask them to play the notes of their original scale, ascending and descending, before beginning the alap.

- After listening to the different alaps, ask the children to describe the sounds and mood of their music.

- Do different scale patterns create different musical effects?

- What is the effect of using long sounds within a piece of music?

- Play the recording of the Indian alap a second time and discuss how it compares with their versions.

# 1: Zum gali gali

Israeli work song

**Resources**

The Green Book

Recording tracks 30 and 31

A large space in which the children can move freely

Two bass or alto xylophones – the lower the pitch the better

**Key vocabulary**

**Ostinato**

Two-part song

**Previous experience**

Singing independent parts.

**OSTINATO**

* Use higher note if no low B is available.

*The Green Book, page 4*

**A** sing

- Teach the song (track 30), by rote, using the Hebrew words if possible. (See page 4 of the Pupils' Book.)

- Ask the children to mime the digging as they sing, imagining they are working hard to plant vegetables.

- Ask some of them to clap on the first beat of each bar.

- Practise until the singing is secure.

**B** sing

- Listen to the second version of the song on track 31. *(This has an ostinato using the words 'zum gali' to create a two-part song.)*

- Divide the class into two groups, with one half singing the ostinato twice as an introduction, before the other half enters with the song. *(See bottom of page 4 of the Pupils' Book.)*

- When the first group has sung through the whole song once, they can take over the ostinato, singing it twice before the second group sings the main melody.

*sing*

- Ask the children to imagine the pioneers starting off from the village to walk to the fields.

- Start the ostinato part quietly and gradually increase the volume *(making a crescendo)* as the pioneers move towards the fields. *(Don't let the children get too loud too soon.)*

- On reaching the fields, the whole song can be sung over the continuing sung ostinato.

- If there is enough space, encourage the children to mime the different jobs they might do in the fields, such as digging, hoeing and planting.

- As the pioneers leave the fields at the end of the day to return to their homes, revert to singing only the ostinato. *(This should get gradually quieter (diminuendo), but might also become gradually slower, representing the weariness of the workers.)*

  *compose*

- Set out two pitched notes, E and B, and ask a child to create a simple ostinato, such as:

- Invite individual children to improvise their own melodies over the E and B ostinato, using this scale.

*(Ensure that there is an F♯ bar on the xylophone which is to be used for improvising a melody.)*

# 2: Repeated patterns

**Resources**

The Green Book

Recording track 32

Tuned and untuned percussion instruments

**Key vocabulary**

**Pentatonic scale**

**Previous experience**

Familiarity with playing percussion instruments.

C pentatonic

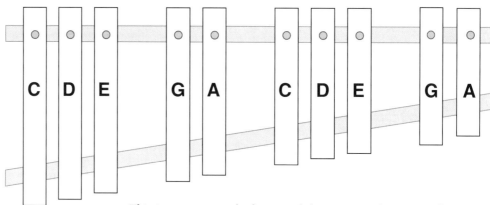

C  D  E  G  A  C

This is a soprano xylophone with bars removed to create the notes of the C pentatonic scale.

The pentatonic scale is a five-note scale with ancient origins. It can be heard in the music of many countries, where it is notated and remembered in different ways. The scale above is written down in traditional western notation.

*The Green Book, page 5*

A   play   sing

- Set out the C pentatonic scale *(see above)* on three or four tuned percussion instruments, making sure that there are two beaters available for each player. *(On some instruments, such as a tenor xylophone, two C scales can be created, enabling two children to use one instrument.)*

- Invite one child to create a short melody as an ostinato using some or all of the notes, which the children can remember and repeat.

- Ask everyone to sing this ostinato.

- Invite another child, playing another instrument, to create a second ostinato which will fit rhythmically with the first one.

- If there are enough instruments (and C pentatonic scales) available, allow up to four children to build on the first ostinato at the same time.

- Repeat the activity with different players, engaging the rest of the class as active listeners, commenting on how well the patterns fit together. (*Give the children time, not only to concentrate on creating their own ostinato patterns, but also to listen to, and fit in with, the other repeated ostinatos.*)

- Ask the listeners to join in and to sing the melodic phrases, to clap the rhythms of the different ostinatos, and to decide the order in which the players should come in. Discuss how and when the players should stop.

- Invite some other children to join in by playing the different rhythms of the ostinatos on untuned percussion instruments.

 **B** listen

- Let the children look at the picture of the African balafon players on page 5 of the Pupils' Book while they listen to the music on track 32.

- Can they hear how the patterns coming in at the beginning?

# 3: Patterns in performance

**Resources**

The Green Book

Keyboards and recorders, and a range of tuned and untuned percussion instruments

Paper and pencils

**Key vocabulary**

**Dynamics**

**Pentatonic**

**Ostinato**

**Structure** (form)

**Previous experience**

Working with pulse, rhythm, and pitch.

Playing, and keeping to, independent parts.

F pentatonic

G pentatonic

*The Green Book, page 5*

- Ask each child to make up and clap a short ostinato rhythm based on their name.
- Choose one of the rhythms and ask everyone to join in clapping the same rhythm. Start quietly, gradually getting louder until everyone is clapping as loudly as they can, then stop.
- Try gradually getting louder and then gradually getting quieter.
- Repeat the activity, this time with the children using their individual ostinatos.
- Ask one child to create and clap an ostinato pattern which fills four beats.
- Ask another child to create and clap a different ostinato pattern which also fills four beats.
- Ask the children to transfer the two patterns on to untuned percussion instruments.

- Ask the children to choose a way of labelling the two different four-beat ostinato patterns, e.g.:

- Let the children decide on a structure for a piece, using the two patterns and including repetition, and write down the pattern of symbols, e.g. ● ● ◆ ◆ ● ●

- Choose two children to play the piece from the symbols.

- Repeat the activity with different children, and a different structure, e.g. ● ◆ ◆ ●

 **B** compose

*Each group of children will need tuned and untuned percussion instruments in order to compose pieces based on ostinato ideas.*

- Ask each group to invent a pattern which fills four beats, and label them as before.

- Encourage the children with tuned instruments, such as xylophones or recorders, to try to make up three short melodic ostinatos using the four-beat patterns, based on the notes of the F and G pentatonic scales on page 5 of the Pupils' Book (and opposite).

- Each group should decide on just one pentatonic scale to use, by playing through all three, so that they can choose the one whose sound they like the best.

- Each group should think carefully about the importance of keeping a steady beat, structuring their piece by deciding who plays when, and using dynamics.

- Play and record the compositions.

 extension activity discuss

- As they listen to each group's composition, encourage the children to analyse the structure (form) of their compositions by writing down the symbols, showing how many times the ostinato patterns are played, and who is playing when, e.g.:

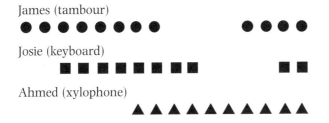

James (tambour)
● ● ● ● ● ● ●      ● ● ● ●

Josie (keyboard)
■ ■ ■ ■ ■ ■ ■      ■ ■

Ahmed (xylophone)
▲ ▲ ▲ ▲ ▲ ▲ ▲ ▲ ▲ ▲

# 1: Sounds from junk

## Resources

The Green Book

Recording tracks 33 and 34

Home-made instruments

Matchboxes of different sizes containing spent matches

Cardboard tubes of different lengths and diameters

Pan lids

Old car hub-caps

Any other junk which can be used to make sounds

## Key vocabulary

Tamboo-bamboo

Steel drum

Skiffle

## Previous experience

Exploring and using different sound sources.

*The Green Book, page 6*

In the West Indies during the 1930s, music was sometimes made on 'junk' instruments such as old biscuit tins, bottles, dustbins and soap-boxes. These musical ensembles were known as 'tamboo-bamboo' bands. The steel drum, which originates from Trinidad, is a good example of the recycling of everyday objects (in this case oil drums) for re-use as musical instruments. Another example of musical recycling is the use of old ridged washboards and tea-chests in the British skiffle bands of the 1950s.

**A**   *discuss*

- Discuss with the children ideas for making junk instruments (see page 6 of the Pupils' Book.)

  Cardboard tubes. (*Strong tubes are best, such as the type used for mailing posters. Different lengths of tube will produce sounds of different pitches when you slap the open end.*)

  Matchboxes, large and small, filled with small articles such as gravel, spent matches. (*The boxes can be tapped and shaken.*)

  Old hub-caps. (*A visit to a car scrap-yard could provide some interesting materials. Hub-caps can be played as metal drums, or suspended to make gongs.*)

  Milk bottles, filled to various levels with water and tapped. (*These produce sounds of different pitch.*)

- Talk about other junk instrument ideas they may have. *(Music can be played on anything that can produce a sound.)*

- Ask the children to find and bring in other objects which could be used as 'junk' instruments *(e.g. pan lids, pieces of wood to tap together, old tins and boxes).*

- Let the children make their own instruments, encouraging them to consider the quality of sound, solidity of structure, and appearance.

**B**  *discuss   play*

*Each child should have a 'junk' instrument.*
- Ask the children to listen to and discuss the sounds which can be produced by their instruments.

  Which instruments make similar sounds and which make different sounds?

  What are the loudest and quietest sounds each instrument can make?

  Who can make the loudest sound, and who can make the quietest?

  How many different ways can they play their instruments?

- Ask them to look at, and compare, the different materials from which the junk is made *(e.g. wood, metal, plastic).*

- Let the children share their sounds and ideas.

- Save all the 'junk' instruments. *(They will be needed for the rest of this Project, and for Project 12.)*

**C**  *listen  discuss*

- Listen to the recording (track 33) in which Benjamin Britten uses drinking mugs to produce his required timbre for the rain sounds. Discuss why he might have chosen a junk instrument. *(e.g. It creates a sound like raindrops.)*

- Listen on track 34 to the steel pan music. Discuss why a steel pan is a junk instrument. *(The pan is made from a discarded oil drum.)*

- Look at and discuss the other junk bands on page 7 of the Pupils' Book.

# 2: Creating a mood

**Resources**

The Green Book

Recording tracks 35–38

A range of untuned percussion instruments

A collection of junk instruments

**Key vocabulary**

**Dynamics**

**Tempo**

**Pitch** (high/low)

**Previous experience**

Playing a range of percussion instruments, using various techniques.

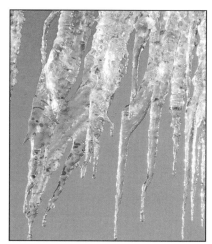

*The Green Book, pages 8 & 9*

 **A** play discuss

- Place some junk instruments and a few tuned and untuned percussion instruments in the middle of the circle.

- Let the children explore some musical opposites (*contrasts of pitch, dynamics, tempo, length, etc.*).

- Invite one child to come into the circle, choose an instrument and play a quiet sound.

- Ask another child to choose another suitable instrument on which to play a contrasting dynamic.

- Let the children decide which instrument might produce a loud sound, or an even quieter sound.

- Repeat the activity, encouraging the children to think of their own musically contrasting ideas (*e.g. rough/smooth, long/short, steady beat/rhythm, fast/slow, high/low, continuous/broken, getting higher/getting lower, metal sound/wooden sound, hard beaters/soft beaters*).

- Try different playing techniques *(e.g. scraping, shaking, tapping)*.

- Give all the children the opportunity to suggest ideas, through both playing and discussing.

- Ask them which instruments they would choose to make contrasting sounds, and to suggest other ideas for creating musical contrasts.

- Try playing the same sound *(e.g. a scraping sound)* on different instruments.

- Encourage them to experiment with playing two contrasting sounds together.

- Ask them to listen to the texture created by a combination of instruments.

**B**    *play discuss*

- Using a range of percussion instruments, ask the children to think of two contrasting emotions or feelings *(e.g. anger and calm, happiness and sadness, boldness and shyness, and any others they can think of)*.

- Invite one child to mime the two emotions and another to accompany the mime on a chosen instrument.

- Ask the children to think about the way emotional language can be used to describe the natural elements, *(e.g. 'Better bring the washing in – it's* **threatening** *rain', 'What a* **gloomy** *day for a picnic', 'There's an* **angry** *storm brewing', 'Better put a coat on, there's a* **cruel** *wind blowing'*.

**C**     *listen discuss*

- In groups, ask the children to choose two contrasting mood pictures from pages 8 and 9 of the Pupils' Book, and make up some music to fit the mood of each one.

- Listen to the four extracts on tracks 35–38, *(Bridge 'The Storm'; Vivaldi 'Winter'; Reich 'Desert Music,' and Vaughan Williams 'The Lark Ascending')*.

- Before discussing the kinds of images the different composers are trying to evoke, allow the children to come to their own conclusions, and discuss their reasons.

- Discuss the ways in which these composers have been inspired by the contrasts and moods of nature. *(Each extract matches with one of the photographs in the Pupils' Book.)*

# 1: The quiet city

**Resources**

The Green Book

Recording track 39

Cassette player

Blank tape

**Key vocabulary**

Atmosphere

Solo

Trumpet

Cor anglais

Strings

**Previous experience**

Active listening to music.

Using the voice in imaginative ways.

Confidence about discussing musical ideas in class.

*The Green Book, page 10*

   **listen** **discuss**

- Ask the children to close their eyes and imagine a quiet scene in a deserted city just before dawn, helping them to put detail into their scenes by asking questions (*e.g. are they seeing a main road through the city, a narrow street, a housing estate, or an open space or park? Is the sky dark? Are the street lights illuminating the roads and buildings? Is it noisy or quiet?*).

- Play the extract from 'Quiet City' and look at the photographs of a city scene on page 10 of the Pupils' Book. Discuss the children's responses to the music.

- Tell them a little about the music (*page 16 of this book*).

- Listen to the music for a second time and ask the children some questions.

    Did anyone recognize any of the instruments? (*Trumpet, cor anglais, (see page 10 of the Pupils' Book), and string orchestra*)

    What was the tempo of the piece being played? (*Slow.*)

    Why has the composer (*Aaron Copland*) written the piece to be played slowly?

    Do the instruments play all together throughout the piece, or are there some solo passages?

**B** *listen discuss*

- Ask the children to close their eyes and sit in silence for 30 seconds, making a mental note of what they hear.

- Was there complete silence? If not, what could they hear?

- Ask them whether they think there is ever absolute silence in the city, and discuss the sounds they might hear. Encourage them to make their sentences as descriptive as possible. (*Description creates atmosphere. Let them look again at the photograph on page 10 of the Pupils' Book.*)

- Write out some descriptive phrases suggested by the children, and ask them to practise saying the sentences in imaginative ways which will create atmosphere.

- Invite them to sit in silence, while one child decides and directs other children to speak each sentence in order, to break up the silence.

**C** *compose*

- Ask the children to create some sound effects which express the descriptive sentences. (*The sound effects may be purely instrumental, including the 'junk' instruments, or be combined with vocal ideas.*)

- Let the children decide when and how the sound effects will be played.

- Ask the children to create their own 'Quiet City' piece. (*In order to create the same uncluttered feel as in Copland's music, suggest that the sound effects be kept separate most of the time – the silences should speak as clearly as the sounds.*)

**Record the work in progress for the next session.**

# 2: The wakening city

**Resources**

The Green Book

Recording tracks 39 and 40

A range of tuned and untuned percussion instruments

Some keyboards

Junk instruments

Recordings of children's work from Project 12, Unit 1

**Key vocabulary**

Transition

Contrast

**Texture**

**Previous experience**

Working within a musical structure.

*The Green Book, page 11*

 **A** *discuss compose*

- Review the ideas worked on in Project 12, Unit 1.

- Ask the children to think about the transition from quiet city to noisy city.
  (*Transition in music is one way a composer moves from one idea to another.*)

- Let them look at the street scenes on page 11 of the Pupils' Book and discuss what is happening.

- Ask them what kinds of sounds would be heard in the city as a new day starts.
  (*They can use the photograph to give them ideas.*)

- Let the children work together on some musical ideas for the transition, using classroom percussion, their junk instruments, and their voices.

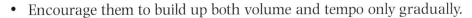

- Encourage them to build up both volume and tempo only gradually.

- Remind them that getting louder does not necessarily mean getting faster.
  *(If they can control dynamics and tempo, the transition passage will be more effective.)*

- Discuss the fact that a denser texture will emerge as the city life gets under way.
  *(At this stage, chaos can be avoided by layering the different ideas and deciding who will play, and when.)*

**B**  listen discuss

- Play the extract from 'Quiet City' (track 39), and 'Ionisation' (track 40).

- Ask the children what immediate differences they notice between the two pieces.
  *(In 'Ionisation' the denser texture leaves no space for silence; the different rhythm and the contrast in dynamics convey an urgent, busy feel to the texture.)*

- What sound can the children hear which is not percussive? *(The siren. This and the tubular bells are shown on page 11 of the Pupils' Book.)*

- As they listen, ask the children to try to identify some of the percussion instruments.

**C**  compose

- Ask the children to create a contrasting piece to their 'Quiet City' music (Unit 1).
  *(They should consider the kinds of instruments they want to use (including junk), and their voices; they should try some short, repeated, rhythmic ideas; they should consider the sound effects it is possible to create, using a keyboard; they should use a range of dynamics.)*

**Record the work in progress.**

# 3: Creation city

**Resources**

The Green Book

A range of tuned and untuned percussion, and junk instruments

Recordings of children's work from Project 12, Unit 2

**Key vocabulary**
**Structure**

**Previous experience**

Performing compositions.

Constructive appraisal of each other's compositions.

## The world

**Looking at the crowded streets**
The sun sinking in the drifting sky
**Looking at my feet as**
The sky begins to darken
With the cool of the night

**Squares of concrete cover the street**
The moon beginning to show its peaceful rays of light
**I look up**
The stars begin to glisten
In the cool of the night

**I smell the air with the stale fumes of smoke**
The moon glowing brightly
With the light of the sun
**And see the lamps that light the world**
While I walk the streets of the world.

*Donald Peters*

*The Green Book, page 12*

**A** *discuss*

- Read the poem 'The world' with the children. *(See page 12 of the Pupils' Book.)*

- Talk about the many contrasts *(such as sky and feet, moon and sun, crowded street and peaceful light.)*

- Point out the contrast of the separate poem which is created by the bold lines.

- Talk about which senses are used in the poem to create mood. *(Sight and smell.)*

- Tell the children they are going to create a piece of music based on their work from the previous units, adding a section about a noisy city.

**B** *compose*

*This extended composition task provides the opportunity for the children to create a structured piece of music made up of two contrasting sections linked by a transition.*

- Discuss with the children the ideas about 'city music' that they have discovered from listening to music, exploring sounds, talking about them, and describing them. They also have recordings of their work in progress to draw upon.

**Section 1. The quiet city**

- Remind the children of the sparse texture. *(They should be careful not to play too many instruments at the same time, so that they can convey the atmosphere of the quiet and empty city.)*

**Transition. The wakening city**

- Ask the children to discuss ways in which the music can gradually be built up *(e.g. by going faster, getting louder, using more instruments, using different instruments).*

**Section 2. The noisy city**

- Remind the children that this section should reflect the busyness and chaos of a crowded city *(e.g. by how the instruments are used, and by introducing rhythmic and non-rhythmic ideas and some unusual sounds).*

- The photograph on page 13 of the Pupils' Book will help them with ideas for this section.

- Appraise the different compositions by performing and discussing them.

*extension activity* *compose*

- The children might like to write poems inspired by their compositions, which can be independent of the music, or can accompany it.

# 1: Trying them out

## Resources

The Green Book

Recording tracks 41 and 42

A range of tuned and untuned percussion instruments, including a large cymbal and a woodblock (ideally, one instrument per child)

A range of hard- and soft-headed beaters – felt, wood, and rubber

Stopwatches, or ordinary watches with second hands

## Key vocabulary

Long, **sustained**, and short sounds

**Timbre**

**Dynamics** – piano/forte, crescendo/diminuendo, mezzo piano/mezzo forte

## Previous experience

Playing tuned and untuned percussion instruments.

Awareness of a range of playing techniques.

Combining sounds to create simple compositions.

gradually **getting** louder *crescendo* or *cresc.*

gradually getting quieter **diminuendo** or *dim.*

a medium quiet sound

mezzo piano

*mp*

a medium loud sound

mezzo forte

*mf*

a quiet sound

piano *p*

a loud sound

forte *f*

*The Green Book, page 14*

**A** play

- Pass a cymbal and beater around the circle and ask each child in turn to think of a different way of playing it *(e.g. fast, slowly, loudly, quietly)*.

- Pass round different types of beaters *(e.g. soft, hard, wire brush. If you have cymbals of different sizes try the same playing technique on each cymbal.)*

- Ask the children to describe the sound quality (timbre) of the different sounds made on the cymbal *(e.g. sharp, rough, smooth, shimmering)*.

- Put a cymbal, a tambour, and a woodblock in the centre of the circle, invite individual children to choose an instrument and think of a way of playing it quietly or loudly.

- Discuss with the children how the way an instrument is struck affects the sound produced. *(Different kinds of playing techniques affect the sound quality.)*

- Try different ways to make the sound gradually get louder or quieter. *(Good physical control is needed when playing any instrument.)*

- Explain that the word 'dynamics' refers to the loudness and quietness of sounds.

- Let the children look at the musical signs for the different dynamics on page 14 of the Pupils' Book.

**B**

- In groups, ask the children, using the stopwatches, to create a crescendo which gradually gets louder over a period of 45–60 seconds.

- Make sure they do not get louder too quickly. *(They might build their crescendo by using different playing techniques, and/or by introducing the instruments at different times. Each player will have to decide how fast to play.)*

- Ask the children to perform and listen to their pieces of music.

- Discuss the similarities and differences.

- Play tracks 41 and 42, and ask the children to listen to the dynamics within these two stylistically very different pieces.

- Discuss the way the crescendo has been built up in each piece.

- Some children may like to create a decrescendo to match their crescendo. *(The music starts loud and gets gradually quieter.)*

- If they are successful in this, they could try linking the two together without a break.

# 2: Time lines

**Resources**

The Green Book

A range of tuned and untuned percussion instruments

Large sheet of plain paper

Graph paper

**Key vocabulary**

**Damping**

**Previous experience**

Awareness of sound and silence in music.

Writing sounds down, using graphic forms of notation.

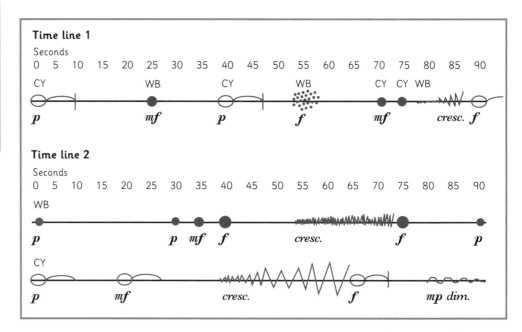

*The Green Book, page 15*

  **A** *discuss*

- Hold up a large piece of blank paper and ask the children to imagine they are going to create a painting.

- Ask them what they must decide before they make the first brush stroke. *(The subject of the painting, the consistency and colour of the paint, the thickness or thinness of the brush, where to make the first mark, how to make the first mark, and how the subject is presented on the sheet.)*

- Now ask the children to compare these decisions with creating a piece of music. *(They need to have an idea of what the piece is about (the subject of the painting) and they must start with silence (the blank piece of paper). They need to plan a good start (the first mark), what sounds to use (the brush strokes), and the overall effect (the complete picture).)*

- While the children look at 'Time line 1' *(on page 15 of the Pupils' Book, and above)*, ask these questions:

  How long does the whole piece last? *(90 seconds.)*

  How long do individual sounds last? *(i.e. the first cymbal sound lasts 10 seconds.)*

  Which dynamic markings can they see in the piece? *(p, mf, f, and cresc.)*

  How many silent sections are there? *(Five.)*

  Where is the cymbal damped? *(10" and 50".)*

**B** *play*

- In pairs, ask the children first to experiment with the sounds their instruments can make. *(Remind them of the effect of colour and line in a painting.)*

- How can they vary their sounds? *(Different ways of using the beaters, contrasting sounds, dynamics.)*

- Ask them to use a time line to compose a piece of music. *(A piece of graph paper may help them to map out the time equally across the page.)*

- Give the children time to compose and write down their pieces, and share the results. *(They could look again at these signs on page 14 of the Pupils' Book.)*

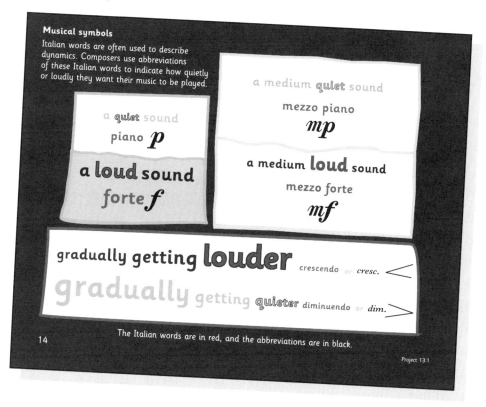

**Musical symbols**
Italian words are often used to describe dynamics. Composers use abbreviations of these Italian words to indicate how quietly or loudly they want their music to be played.

a **quiet** sound
piano *p*

a **loud** sound
forte *f*

a medium **quiet** sound
mezzo piano
*mp*

a medium **loud** sound
mezzo forte
*mf*

gradually getting **louder** crescendo or *cresc.*

gradually getting quieter diminuendo or *dim.*

The Italian words are in red, and the abbreviations are in black.

14

Project 13·1

*extension activity*  *compose*

- Ask the children to look at 'Time line 2' for cymbal and woodblock on page 15 of the Pupils' Book (and opposite), and create a piece based on this.

# 3: *Sounds together*

**Resources**

The Green Book

Recording tracks 43 and 44

A range of tuned and untuned percussion instruments

A keyboard and any other suitable sound makers

**Key vocabulary**

**Texture**

**Timbre**

**Previous experience**

Knowledge of a range of playing techniques and experience of working with sounds.

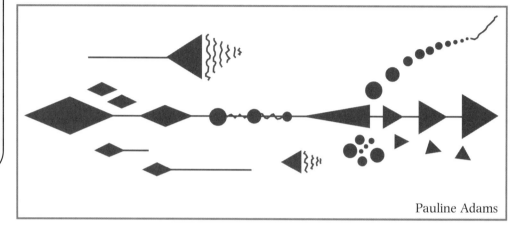

Pauline Adams

*The Green Book, page 17*

    **A** play discuss

- Introduce the activity by telling the children they are going to create a piece together by improvising on their instruments.

- Ask for a volunteer conductor who will control the playing of the class by giving signals to start and stop, and make sure the children know what the signs are.

- Let the conductor practise his or her stop and start signals so that everyone understands them.

- Tell the children they may only make quiet sounds on their instruments.

- Ask the children whether they thought that the conductor's signals were clear.

- Can they think of some more useful signals for the conductor to use?

- Ask them to think about signals for individuals to start and stop playing, for playing short sounds or continuous sounds, for changing dynamics *(e.g. suddenly louder, getting quieter)*, for changing the tempo, *(e.g. starting slowly, then gradually getting faster)*, for silent sections.

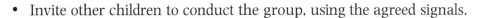

- Invite other children to conduct the group, using the agreed signals.
- Discuss their conducted improvisations.

    Were the signals clear?

    Did the players respond accurately to the signals?

    Which instruments, if any, were prominent?

    Was there a good balance of sound?

    Could all the instruments be heard?

    Did the piece feel too long, too short, or just the right length?

(B)    *play*

- Repeat activity 1, suggesting that the conductors give the players more specific verbal instructions before they play *(e.g. play the xylophones with fingertips, play the drum with wooden-headed beaters, use a particular 'voice' on the keyboard, improvise on keyboards and wooden tuned percussion using only certain pitched notes).*

- Play tracks 43 (CD 1) and 44 (CD 2), (see page 17) and ask the children to listen to the timbre and texture created by the instruments in the two pieces, both of which involve percussion playing. *(The instruments used are shown on page 16 of the Pupils' Book.)*

- Ask them to listen to the way the kettle drum changes pitch in 'The road is wider than long' *(the pedal on the drum changes the tension of the skin).*

- Ask them to listen for the rhythmic interest within 'Second construction', and also for the use of dynamics.

- Ask them, remembering their own time line compositions, whether these extracts could be written out in a similar way.

*extension activity*    *play*

- Let the children look at the graphic score on page 17 of the Pupils' Book (see opposite page), and ask them to carry out the task for themselves. *(They should discuss how they might do this, and which instruments they might use. The number of players in any group should not exceed six.)*

# 1: Dhum tak

**Resources**

The Green Book

Recording
track 45

A variety of drums

**Key vocabulary**

Darabuka (drum)

**Previous experience**

Exploring the range of sounds which can be made on a drum.

Awareness of the existence of different ways of notating music.

*The **darabuka** originated in the Middle East. In Egypt it is known as a tabl, and in Iran as a zarb.*

*The Green Book, page 18*

   **A** listen

- Ask the children to look at the picture of a darabuka drum on page 18 of the Pupils' Book, and listen to the recording (track 45) of the rhythm played on a darabuka. *(There are eight beats in this repeated drum pattern, made up of low and high sounds. This rhythmic style is known as 'masmoudi'. The low sound, produced by playing with the flat of the hand and bouncing it off the surface of the middle of the drum, has the mnemonic name 'dhum'. The high sound, which is produced by playing on the edge, or rim of the drum with one finger, is called 'tak'.)*

- Ask the children to listen to the masmoudi rhythm again. Can they hear on which beats the dhum is sounded? *(1, 2, and 5 – see below).*

| 1 | 2 | 3 | 4 | 5 | 6 | 7 | 8 |
|------|------|---|---|------|---|---|---|
| dhum | dhum | | | dhum | | | |

**B**  play

- Place a variety of drums, including tambours, in the centre of the circle.

- Invite individual children to choose a drum and find the lowest sound it will make *(the dhum)*, and then to find and play a high sound *(the tak)*. The simplest form of the eight-beat pattern of the masmoudi rhythm is divided into the following dhums and taks:

| 1 | 2 | 3 | 4 | 5 | 6 | 7 | 8 |
|---|---|---|---|---|---|---|---|
| dhum | dhum | tak | tak | dhum | tak | tak | tak |

- Ask the children to speak this pattern several times and try to memorize it.

- Ask them to try playing it, by tapping knees on the 'dhums', tapping fingers on palms for the 'taks'.

- Invite some children, one at a time, to choose a drum and play the 'dhum' and 'tak' sounds, by using high and low playing techniques.

**C**  play

- Tell the children that another masmoudi sound is 'taka' which is another high sound, produced by tap.

- Ask the children to try saying this second pattern several times until they have memorized it:

| 1 | 2 | 3 | 4 | 5 | 6 | 7 | 8 |
|---|---|---|---|---|---|---|---|
| dhum | dhum | taka | taka | dhum | tak | taka | tak |

- Ask the children in pairs to create a new eight-beat pattern made up of 'dhums', 'taks', and 'takas'. *(They must keep the 'dhums' on beats one, two and five to retain the masmoudi structure. They should speak their pattern first, as this helps them to memorize it.)*

- Let them practise their patterns by tapping the different sounds in different ways.

- Perform the patterns, listening for identical or similar patterns.

- Invite the children to transfer the patterns on to drums. *(Make sure there are clear differences between the dhums, taks, and takas.)*

- Ask two or three children each to try playing a different pattern at the same time.

*(The children can see the two rhythms from this activity, and activity B, on page 18 of the Pupils' Book.)*

# 2: Dha dhin dhin

**Resources**
The Green Book
Recording tracks
46, 47, 48 and 49

A variety of drums
and untuned
percussion

**Key vocabulary**
Tabla (drums)
Harmonium
**Tal** (rhythm pattern)
**Bol** (tabla
mnemonic)

**Previous
experience**
Using a range
of techniques
to produce
different sounds
on instruments.

Experience of playing
different beat
groupings.

*The Green Book, page 19*

   **A** listen

- Let the children listen to the recording (track 46) made in Calcutta, India. *(Two tabla players are practising together.)*

- Ask the children to listen for what happens when the tabla players stop playing their rhythm. *(One of the players talks very fast and rhythmically, saying complicated rhythmic patterns which they have learnt and memorized. Each syllable is a bol – a mnemonic such as 'dha' – which represents one of the many different sounds that can be produced on the tabla.)*

- Remind the children of the way they played two sounds, dhum and tak in Unit 1. The tabla players do not use the words dhum and tak; they use other mnemonics, to represent a more extensive range of sounds.

- Ask the children to look at the pictures on pages 18 and 19 of the Pupils' Book. What are the main differences between the darabuka and the tabla? *(Tabla are two drums of differing sizes; they can therefore be played separately or together. They are very different in shape from the darabuka, and are played sitting on the floor.)*

**B**    listen

- Ask the children to listen to the recording (track 47) of a simple pattern of sounds. *(The sounds are first spoken and then played. The whole pattern spans 16 beats, a common tal (time cycle) in Indian Music.)*

- Can the children remember from the recording any of the spoken syllables (bols)? *(Dha, dhin, ta, and tin.)*

- Play the recording again, and ask them to listen to the way the four different bol sounds are spoken and then played.

- Ask them which bol represent the low, and which the high sounds. *(Dha and dhin are the low sounds made on both drums; ta and tin are higher sounds, made only on the small tabla.)*

- Practise saying the syllables of the 16-beat cycle.

| 1 | 2 | 3 | 4 | 5 | 6 | 7 | 8 | 9 | 10 | 11 | 12 | 13 | 14 | 15 | 16 |
|---|---|---|---|---|---|---|---|---|---|---|---|---|---|---|---|
| dha | dhin | dhin | dha | dha | dhin | dhin | dha | dha | tin | tin | ta | ta | dhin | dhin | dha |

- Can the children memorize it in the same way as the tabla players do? *(Play the recording again and ask the children to join in with the words. If they need help to memorize it they can look at pattern 1 at the bottom of page 19 of the Pupils' Book).*

extension activity   listen

- *The 16-beat pattern (or tal) they have just learnt has a particular name. It is called Tintal.*

- Listen to the recording on track 48. This is a more complicated pattern, using three more bols (tere, kete, tu, and na).

| 1 | 2 | 3 | 4 | 5 | 6 | 7 | 8 | 9 | 10 | 11 | 12 | 13 | 14 | 15 | 16 |
|---|---|---|---|---|---|---|---|---|---|---|---|---|---|---|---|
| dha | dha | tere | kete | dha | dha | tu | na | ta | ta | tere | kete | ta | ta | tu | na |

- Let a few children learn this pattern *(if they need help they can see this second tal on page 19 of the Pupils' Book)* then let the class try saying both patterns at the same time, being careful about keeping a steady pulse, and fitting the two-syllable words against the single syllable words.

| 1 | 2 | 3 | 4 | 5 | 6 | 7 | 8 | 9 | 10 | 11 | 12 | 13 | 14 | 15 | 16 |
|---|---|---|---|---|---|---|---|---|---|---|---|---|---|---|---|
| dha | dhin | dhin | dha | dha | dhin | dhin | dha | dha | tin | tin | ta | ta | dhin | dhin | dha |
| dha | dha | tere | kete | dha | dha | tu | na | ta | ta | tere | kete | ta | ta | tu | na |

- Now listen to track 49. The children will first hear the basic Tintal pattern being played and then a second player will join in saying and playing the second, more complicated pattern.

# 1: *Panamam tombé*

West Indian calypso

**Resources**

The Green Book

Recording
track 50

**Key vocabulary**

Off-**beat**

**Calypso**

**Previous experience**

Playing a rhythmic
accompaniment to
a song, keeping
a steady beat.

Teachers who play the guitar may wish to use the chord of C⁷ instead of C. (See chord chart on page 154.)

The song is written out in full on page 20 of the Pupils' Book. This song is composed in a **calypso** style and originates from the West Indies. The use of the French word 'tombé' (fall) may indicate that the song originated from one of the islands which were at one time occupied by the French.

*The Green Book, page 20*

**A**  *sing*

- Ask the children to listen to and start learning the song on page 20 of the Pupils' Book.

- Do any of the children know that a 'panama' is a type of straw hat?

- Ask them if they notice a difference between the first and second times they sing 'tombé'. *(The first 'Panamam tombé' moves in an upward direction, finishing on a high note, and the second moves in a downward direction, finishing on a low note.)*

- What do they notice about the phrases beginning, 'Please pick up my panama' and 'When I left the carnival'? *(They are the same, except that the second phrase starts one note lower.)*

*Listening to and talking about the shape of the music will help the children to memorize the song accurately.*

**B**  *play*

- Ask the children to count steadily from 1 to 8. *(There are 8 quavers in each bar of the song.)*

- When they can do this steadily, ask them to clap every time they say '1'.

| | 1 | 2 | 3 | 4 | 5 | 6 | 7 | 8 |
|---|---|---|---|---|---|---|---|---|
| Group | X | | | | | | | |

- Next, ask them to try clapping on '1' and invite them to choose one other number to clap on, *(e.g. 1 and 6).*

| | 1 | 2 | 3 | 4 | 5 | 6 | 7 | 8 |
|---|---|---|---|---|---|---|---|---|
| Group | X | | | | | X | | |

- Try some other combinations, but always clap on beat 1.

**C**  *play*

- Divide the class in two, with Group 1 tapping the beat, and Group 2 clapping the rhythm.

| | 1 | 2 | 3 | 4 | 5 | 6 | 7 | 8 |
|---|---|---|---|---|---|---|---|---|
| Group 1 | X | X | X | X | X | X | X | X |
| Group 2 | X | | | X | | | X | |

- Invite some of the children to clap the calypso rhythm as an accompaniment to the song. *(The 8 beats fit the 8 quavers in each bar of the song.)*

# 2: *Bongo rhythm*

**Resources**
The Green Book
Recording
track 51
Tuned and
untuned
percussion
instruments,
including
bongos and
congas

**Key vocabulary**
**Syncopation**/Off-beat
**Calypso**
Accompaniment

**Previous experience**
Using two beaters on
the tuned percussion
instruments.

Knowing the song
Panamam tombé
(Project 15, Unit 1).

*The Green Book, page 21*

**A**   *sing* *play*

- Revise and sing 'Panamam tombé' from the previous unit (page 98).

- Consider, with the children, any difficulties, and practise any phrases which are still insecure.

- Let the children practise the rhythmic accompaniment they learnt in two groups at the end of the last unit.

- Now ask the children to practise the following bongo rhythm. This requires a two-hand technique, tapping on their knees. *(See page 21 of the Pupils' Book.)*

|  | 1 | 2 | 3 | 4 | 5 | 6 | 7 | 8 |
|---|---|---|---|---|---|---|---|---|
| **Right hand** |  | ● | ● |  | ● | ● |  | ● |
| **Left hand** | ●<br>> |  |  | ●<br>> |  |  | ●<br>> |  |

> = accent

- Ask the children to notice how the eight beats are divided up into two groups of three and one group of two. *(The left hand plays on beats one, four, and seven.)*

- Point out to the children that the left hand pattern of this rhythm is the same as the rhythm that group 2 played in the previous unit.

Here is the bongo rhythm written in traditional western notation:

*(Using bongo drums will give the player the option of playing two different pitches.)*

- Ask the children to sing 'Panamam tombé' with the bongo accompaniment, tapping their knees, using bongos, or playing two small drums of different sizes.

**B**  **listen**

- Let the children listen to 'Jamaican rumba' (track 51), and look at the carnival picture on page 21 of the Pupils' Book.

- Can they hear that the opening section of the piece uses the same calypso-style rhythm as they played when accompanying 'Panamam tombé'? *(The rhythm is divided between the left and right hands in exactly the same way as the bongo rhythm on page 21 of the Pupils' Book.)*

- Have any children been to a carnival like the one in the picture? What kind of music did they hear?

**extension activity**  **play**

*'Panamam tombé' can be accompanied with the following two chords (and see page 21 of the Pupils' Book):*

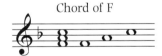

Chord of F

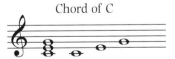

Chord of C

- Let three children play each chord on tuned percussion.

- The song on page 20 of the Pupils' Book shows where the chords are played.

*Some children may enjoy the challenge of playing the chords on the keyboard.*

# 1: Rhythmic division

**Resources**

Three flash cards (see adjacent diagrams)

Photocopied grids (see page 156)

Scissors and glue

A range of tuned and untuned percussion instruments

**Key vocabulary**

**Beat**

**Accent**

**Cross-rhythm**

**Previous experience**

Working with beat and rhythm.

Inventing rhythms.

Using accents.

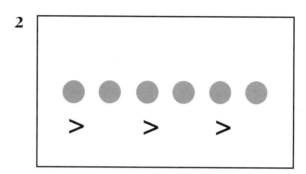

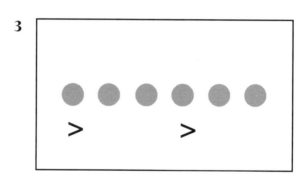

**Make three flash cards as above.**

*Cross-rhythms are created by grouping the same number of beats in different ways. Accents (>) are what define the beat groupings. The activities combine two simple beat divisions to create a cross-rhythm.*

- Ask the children to repeat the numbers 1 to 6 a number of times. *(Set the speed of the pulse first, and make sure the children keep a steady beat.)*

- Show the children flash card 1 and let them clap the beats, accenting the first beat. Repeat this several times.

- Hold up flash cards 2 and 3, and ask the children to look for the accented notes. Ask them how many accents are on each card, and which beats they are under.

- Tell the children that the accents divide the six beats into two different groupings. Ask them how many groups of notes there are on each card. (*Three on card 2, two on card 3.*)

- Ask the children to decide on the speed of the pulse and then play card 2 a number of times, clapping the accented notes and tapping the knees on the others.

- Do the same thing with card 3, at the same tempo.

- Practise playing and repeating each grouping at different tempos, invite the children to decide on the speed.

- When this is secure, split the class into two groups and play both cards together. (*Make sure that the accents can be heard.*)

- Change over groups. (*You could let half the class listen, while the other half performs in two groups.*)

**B**   compose

- Working in pairs, give each pair a sheet of grids (page 156).

- Using at least 4 of their 6 grids, ask them to use the grids to compose a short structured piece. They should experiment by cutting out and placing the sections in different sequences until they decide on the final order.

- Let them practise and perform their piece using body sounds or untuned percussion instruments. (*The accents can be made in different ways, e.g. by making a louder sound, or a different sound.*)

- They should stick down their paper grids to make a score of their music. (*This will ensure that they will be able to remember their pieces.*)

extension activity  compose

- The children could devise 6-beat grids, using blank paper, incorporating rests into the two and three group patterns, to create more interesting pieces, e.g.

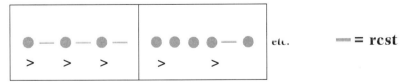

# 2: Cross-rhythm

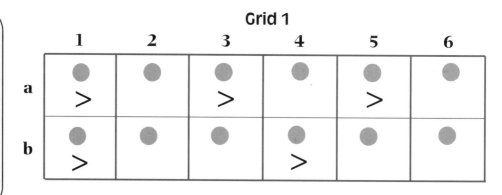

Resources

The Green Book

Recording tracks 52, 53, and 54

A range of untuned percussion instruments

Grids 1 and 2 on separate sheets

**Key vocabulary**

**Cross-rhythm**

**Accent**

Arrangement

**Previous experience**

Working with different beat groupings.

Arranging music for percussion instruments.

## Grid 1

|   | 1 | 2 | 3 | 4 | 5 | 6 |
|---|---|---|---|---|---|---|
| a | ● > | ● | ● > | ● | ● > | ● |
| b | ● > | ● | ● | ● > | ● | ● |

## Grid 2

|   | 1 | 2 | 3 | 4 | 5 | 6 |
|---|---|---|---|---|---|---|
| c | ● > | ● | ● > |   | ● > |   |
| d | ● > |   | ● | ● > |   |   |

**Photocopies of these grids can be made from page 157.**

*The Green Book, page 22*

### Jump and shout

| 1 | 2 | 3 | 4 | 5 | 6 |
|---|---|---|---|---|---|
| I'll > | keep | the | beat > | stea —— dy | |
| Jump > | | and > | | shout > | |
| High > | | | life! > | | |
| Move/ groove > | | | | | and |

*The Green Book, page 23*

**A** listen

- Ask the children to listen to the recording on track 52. Can they hear how many instruments are playing? *(Two.)*

- Let them look at the pictures on page 22 of the Pupils' Book and decide which instruments are playing. *(Small drum and gong bell.)*

- Play track 52 again and point to Grid 1. Ask the children which instrument is playing line (a) *(small drum)*, and which is playing line (b) *(gong bell)*.

- Ask them if they know how the accents are made. *(The gong player accents beats by playing a lower sound, and the drum player by playing louder.)*

- Repeat this activity with Grid 2, track 53. *(Line (c) is played by the shekere, and line (d) by the large drum. The accents on the shekere are created by tapping it on the knee, and on the drum by hitting it on the edge instead of the middle.)*

- Ask the children if they have noticed that there are rests in both grids.

- Ask one child to hold up Grid 1, and a second child to hold up Grid 2 while they listen to the recording on track 54. *(This piece uses all four of the rhythms shown on Grids 1 and 2. Sometimes each grid rhythm is played separately, and sometimes both are played together.)*

- Invite the children to point to whichever grid they can hear, pointing with both hands if they can hear both rhythms.

**B** sing

- Teach the class the 'Jump and shout' chant opposite and on page 23 of the Pupils' Book. *(Learn each line separately, repeating it several times, then try putting the parts together when each line is secure. The bottom line should be chanted as 'Move ...... and'.)*

- In groups, ask the children to play the rhythms of 'Jump and shout' on their choice of percussion instruments, first letting them decide who is going to play each line and agreeing on the speed of the pulse.

- Invite them to practise all the lines together, repeating the grid several times. *(The bottom line becomes 'Move ...... and groove ...... and move ......, etc.)*

- Finally, let them decide how to structure the repeats *(e.g. the instruments come in one at a time, they all get louder, and everybody stops on an agreed signal).* Then perform and record the different arrangements, then play the recordings. Can the listeners hear each individual part, and can they hear the accented beats clearly?

# 3: *High life*

### Resources

The Green Book

A two-pitched metal instrument, (e.g. gong bell, agogo bell, or two chime bars)

Shekere, maraca, cane rattles, cabasa

A variety of drums

Recording tracks 55, 56, and 57

### Key vocabulary

Accompaniment

**Ensemble**

### Previous experience

Working with different beat groupings

Music and words: Pauline Adams

CHORUS

Dance to the mu-sic, dance to the mu - sic, dance and sing.

VERSE

1. High life to feel the beat, high life to move and groove to.

**CHORUS:**

*Dance to the music ...*

**2. High life to jump and shout, high life to move and groove to (repeat)**

*Dance to the music ...*

**3. High life to touch the sun, high life to move and groove to (repeat)**

*Dance to the music ...*

*The Green Book, page 24*

**A** listen sing

- Ask the children to listen to version 1 of the song 'High life' (track 55).

- Play the track again while they follow the music at the top of page 24 of the Pupils' Book. Ask the children how the beats are grouped in the chorus *(groups of two)*, and in the verse *(groups of three)*.

- Sing through the song, incorporating the claps as marked.

**B** listen sing

- Play version 2 of 'High life' (track 56), and ask the children to listen out for the drum accompaniment.

- Ask the children to practise the drum part from the accompaniment score on page 24 of the Pupils' Book, using their left and right hands as shown, on bongos or on their knees.

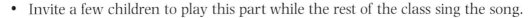

- Invite a few children to play this part while the rest of the class sing the song.

- Listen to version 3 of 'High life' (track 57), and ask the children how many more instruments are playing. (*Two, the gong bell and shekere.*)

- Ask the children what they notice about these two parts. (*They both play the same steady beat, but in the verse the gong bell plays lower and higher sounds.*)

- Look at the accompaniment score again, to see how all the parts fit together.

- Sing the song and practise adding all the accompaniment parts on suitable percussion instruments.

- After performing the piece, ask the children if they think that their singing and instrument accompaniment balance each other (*i.e. neither part being too loud*).

- Let the children decide on more interesting ways of starting and finishing the accompaniment and the song (*i.e. making up an introduction, fading away at the end*).

- Perform the finished version.

*extension activity* *play*

- Ask some of the children who are able, to play the accompaniment purely as an ensemble piece, this time involving more instruments, or using clapping and tapping sounds. They should use the lower three lines of this score on page 24 of the Pupils' Book.

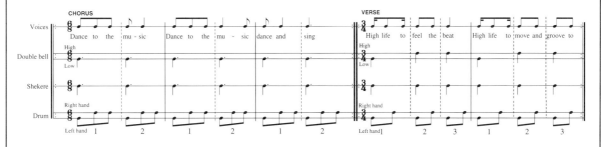

# 1: Comic capers

**Resources**
The Purple Book
Recording
track 58
Paper and pencil

**Key vocabulary**
Onomatopoeia
**Dynamics**
**Pitch**

**Previous experience**
A variety of vocal work.

*The Purple Book, page 1*

   **A** *sing*

- Ask the children to say together the sound 'Sh', as quickly as possible. *(They will need a start signal.)*

- Ask each child in turn to say 'Sh', passing it around the circle as quickly as possible.

- Invite all the children together to say 'Shhhhh', making the sound as long as possible. *(They should use one breath, then stop.)*

- Pass the long 'Shhhhh' around the circle.

- Repeat, making the sound continuous by overlapping it.

**B**  *sing*

- Ask the children to look at the words on the left-hand side of page 1 of the Pupils' Book (and opposite).

- Ask them why the words have been written in this way. *(To convey their meaning and mood.)*

- Introduce the word 'onomatopoeia', and ask the children to think of ways in which some of the words could be said *(e.g. 'bubble' could be whispered, 'vroom' could go from low to high, 'splat' could emphasize each consonant).*

- Ask each child to think of a vocal sound, and invite each child to perform their sound around the circle; the one who starts should decide whether to perform the sound loudly or quietly.

- The next child performs their sound using the opposite dynamic.

- Repeat the exercise, this time using alternate high and low pitches.

- Let the children try to write down the words that they have been experimenting with, to show how they want them to be said. *(They could try their words out on a partner to see if the words are interpreted in the way they hoped.)*

- Keep this work for future use.

**C**  *listen*

- Let the children listen to 'Stripsody' on track 58.

- Ask the children in what ways the singer Cathy Berberian changes her voice. *(By using different tone qualities, by moving faster and slower, and by getting higher and lower.)*

# 2: Comic strips

**Resources**

The Purple Book

Recording track 58

Comics (ask the children to bring these in before the lesson)

**Key vocabulary**

**Improvise**

**Previous experience**

Using graphic notation.

*The Purple Book, page 1*

 **A** *sing*

- Ask the children to look at some words found in the comics they have brought in *(and see right-hand side of page 1 of the Pupils' Book, and above)*, and choose one word *(e.g. 'splat!')*.

- Ask each child in turn to say the word in their own way *(e.g. high/low, rising/falling, fast/slow, loud/quiet, emphasizing vowels or consonants)*.

- Choose one or two other words and pass them round the circle, voicing them in different ways.

- Repeat the activity, allowing the children, if they wish, to change their word or their performance of it.

- Let them practise until each child is satisfied with the result.

- Ask the children to be sure that they know the sound of the word chosen by the person on their right, then ask them to close their eyes and perform clockwise around the circle. *(This activity requires much concentration.)*

**B** sing

- Invite one of the children to be the conductor and direct the sounds to improvise a piece of music.

- Ask the children to keep to their chosen word and the way they have decided to perform it, but this time the conductor determines when each word shall be performed. Here are some possibilities:

    Choose a number of sounds which begin with the same letter, and string them together. *(It will help if the children performing these words are sitting together.)*

    Ask the conductor to change the speed of the improvisation, so that sometimes the words follow on quickly from one another, and at other times there is a gap or silence between them.

- Repeat the activity, this time choosing contrasting sounds.

**C** compose

- Ask the children to look at page 2 of the Pupils' Book for some comic strip ideas.

- Ask them to work in groups on a vocal composition, using one of these ideas, such as 'Getting up in the morning', as a score, or inventing one of their own. The composition may either tell a story or create an atmosphere.

- Encourage them to use the ideas they have used in this and the previous session. *(It might help them to listen to 'Stripsody' again, on track 58.)*

- Record their work for use in the next unit.

# 3: Comic voices

**Resources**

The Purple Book

Recording track 58

Large sheets of paper and drawing materials

**Key vocabulary**

**Graphic score**

**Previous experience**

Project 17, Unit 2.

Using graphic notation.

Awareness of pitch direction.

High-pitched sounds

Medium-pitched sounds

Low-pitched sounds

**Stripsody by Cathy Berberian**

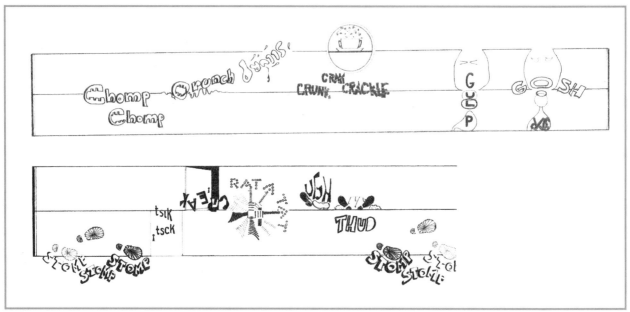

**Stripsody** Edition Peters No. 66164 © 1996 by C. Peters Corporation, New York. Reprinted by permission of Peters Edition Limited, London.

*The Purple Book, page 3*

**A** _listen_

- Ask the children to look at the extract from the score of 'Stripsody' on page 3 of the Pupils' Book, while they listen to the recorded excerpt on track 58.

- Play the recording again, and ask the children to look carefully to see how the score represents the sounds that they can hear.

- Ask them to think about possible ways of writing down the vocal sounds from the piece they composed and recorded in Unit 2 _(e.g. how will they show different pitch levels and dynamics? They can use ideas from the words they wrote in Unit 1 and from the 'Stripsody' score)._

  **B** _compose_

- Working in the same composition groups that they were in for Unit 2, encourage them to use their imagination and drawing skills to create a graphic score for their comic strip pieces. _(They will need time to discuss, experiment, write, and refine their work.)_

- Let them look at the symbols and graphic scores from units 1 and 2 of Project 13 'Sounds extended' on pages 14 and 15 of the The Green Pupils' Book _(see below)._

   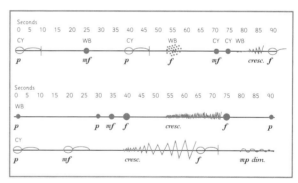

- Perform, discuss, and compare the compositions and scores.

  _extension activity_

- Some children may wish to develop further the art work aspect of the task, and produce scores which use different artistic techniques, such as the use of different materials (paint, crayon, pencil), the use of graphics, pattern, texture, and colour, and the use of shape, form, and space.

# 1: Chairs to mend

**Resources**

The Purple Book

Recording tracks 59 and 60

**Key vocabulary**

Three-part

Street cries

**Previous experience**

Singing simple ostinato accompaniments.

Traditional song

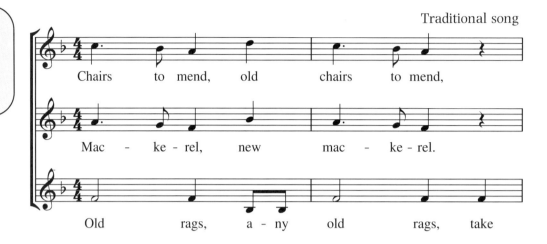

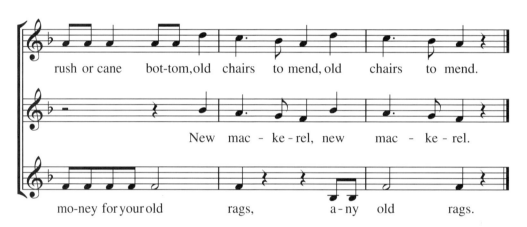

This three-part round, based on street cries, is best learnt one part at a time.

*The Purple Book, page 4*

   *listen*

- Ask the children to listen to 'Chairs to mend' (track 59) several times. *(This will give them time to make sense of the whole piece.)* Discuss the following points:

  How many singers can they hear? *(Three.)*

  What are the songs about? *(Selling things in the street.)*

  What are the cries about? *(1. Chairs to mend 2. New mackerel 3. Old rags.)*

- Let the children look at the pictures of the street sellers on pages 4 and 5 of the Pupils' Book.

**B**   sing

- Teach each of the street cries from the song on page 4 of the Pupils' Book to a different group of children.

- Ask them to imagine they are advertising their goods and skills in the street. *(They need to project their voices in such a way as to attract the attention of passers-by.)*

- Invite each group to sing their cry separately, starting with the 'Chairs to mend' group.

- If this goes well, ask the children to try fitting the three cries together, each group singing their cry a number of times. *(Watch out for rests! If the children find this difficult, ask them to mark the rests with a silent hand gesture.)*

- Ask them to move around as they sing their cries. *(This provides an opportunity for some dramatic interpretation.)*

**C**   sing

- Ask the children to swap the cries around, so that each group practises each cry.

- When they feel secure with all three parts, invite them to try singing the whole round all the way through, together in unison.

- Next, invite them to try singing the round in three parts. *(Each part starts at the beginning and sings all the way through the three sections of the round.)*

**D**   listen

- Ask the children to listen to the 'The Cryes of London' on track 60.

- Ask them to listen for the different things that are being sold *(e.g. walnuts, haddock, ink).*

- Can they say anything about the singers? *(The cries are sung by both men and women.)*

- What else can be heard in the piece? *(Stringed instruments.)*

# 2: Street cries

**Resources**

The Purple Book

Recording tracks 60 and 61

**Key vocabulary**

**Pitch**

**Notation**

**Previous experience**

Singing rounds.

Keeping independent parts.

Hot     cod - lings     hot

New   had - docks   new

New   mus - sels, new   li - ly - white   mus - sels

Buy   a - ny   ink   will you buy   a - ny   ink

God   give you good   mor - row   my   mas - ters,   past   three o' clock

*The Purple Book, pages 4 & 5*

**A** listen

- Let the children listen again to 'The Cyres of London', by Orlando Gibbons, on track 60.

    How many notes are used for the cry 'God give you ...'? *(One note – D.)*

    Can they remember any of the other cries from the extract and work out how many notes were used for each? *(The notated cries are shown above and on pages 4 and 5 of the Pupils' Book.)*

- Let them try singing some of the cries.

**B**    *sing*

- In pairs ask the children to invent their own street cries. *(They may wish to use old-style cries as notated below the pictures on pages 4 and 5 of the Pupils' Book, or make up cries set in a more modern context, e.g. hamburgers, ice-cream, hot dogs, newspapers. There are some ideas on the right of the picture.)*

- Remind them to keep their cries 'punchy' and short, pitching them so that they can be clearly heard. *(The cries need only a few notes, but make sure the tunes are all different.)*

- Ask them to pretend to be street criers, pointing out that gestures and facial expressions would be as important in the selling of goods as the cry itself. *(Children who feel shy or reticent about singing on their own may work better with a partner.)*

- Invite the class to share and discuss their ideas.

    Do any of the cries fit well together?

    Try overlapping some of them.

    What about a collage of cries?

**C**    *listen*

- Let the children listen to track 61 (the Berio 'Cries of London'), and discuss the music.

- Do the children think the piece was written a long time ago or more recently? *(Recently – old themes can always be explored in new ways.)* These are the words of the extract.

Money, penny come to me
I sell old clothes,
For one penny, for two pennies
Old clothes to sell.

If I had such money as I could tell
I would never cry
Old clothes to sell.

- Play the Orlando Gibbons cries again (track 60).

    What are the main differences between the two? *(The voices are accompanied by stringed instruments in the Gibbons, and are unaccompanied in the Berio.*

    *In the Gibbons each voice enters separately, and there is occasional overlapping of the different cries, whereas in the Berio the singers sing together and individually.*

    *The singers in the Gibbons sing straight phrases and sentences, but in the Berio there is more emphasis on exploring individual words.)*

# 1: Drunken sailor

**Resources**

The Purple Book

Recording
track 62

Alto xylophone

**Key vocabulary**

Verse/chorus

**Chord**

**Melody**

**Previous
experience**

Playing and using
chords, as in Project 8.

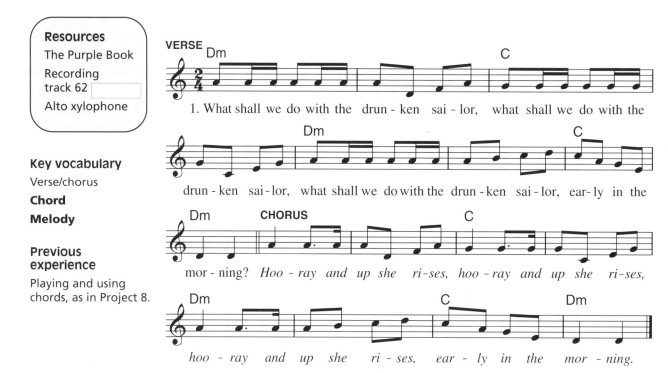

There is a piano accompaniment for this song on page 149.

## What shall we do with the drunken sailor?

2. Put him in the longboat until he's sober,
   put him in the longboat until he's sober,
   put him in the longboat until he's sober,
   early in the morning.
   *Hooray ...*

3. Put him in the scuppers with the hose pipe on him,
   put him in the scuppers with the hose pipe on him,
   put him in the scuppers with the hose pipe on him,
   early in the morning.
   *Hooray ...*

*The Purple Book, page 6*

*This was a favourite 'runaway' shanty sung in the days of the large sailing ships. It was sung by all the sailors as they 'ran away' with the braces (ropes), swinging the yards (wooden booms) round while tacking (changing the direction of) the ship. Longboat = a small boat to take the crew to shore or to other big boats. Scuppers = the holes where water drained off the deck.*

**A**  *discuss sing*

- Ask the children to listen to the recording of the song on track 62 and to look at page 6 of the Pupils' Book. Discuss the purpose and meaning of the song, setting it into historical context.

  *When and why were sailing ships important in history? (For exploration to new lands and continents, e.g. Drake and Raleigh in Tudor times; in wars, e.g. the Armada of 1588; for trade, e.g. the tea clippers of the 1850s.)*

On what occasions might the song have been sung? *(When sailors were pulling on the ship's ropes to raise the sails or the anchor.)*

Why might the sailors have wanted to sing? *(To help them pull together on the beat, as this would give them maximum pulling effect. To relieve the tedium of a hard, boring job.)*

Why don't sailors need to sing work songs like this now? *(Because in a ship driven by engines, power winches pull on the cables.)*

- Learn and sing the song, noticing the strong work-style in which it is sung.
- What do the children notice about the words and rhythm of the verse? *(The first three phrases use the same words and have the same rhythm.)*
- Ask them to clap the rhythm of the verse.
- Ask what is different about the last phrase, 'early in the morning'.
  *(It uses different words and has a different rhythm.)*
- Ask them to clap *this* rhythm together.
- Ask the children what they notice about the melody of the whole song.
  *(The melody of the chorus is the same as that of the song. The shape of the melody in the second 'what shall we do with the drunken sailor' is the same as that of the first, but it starts one note lower. It might help to play the two shapes on an instrument to make it clearer.)*

First phrase
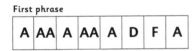

Second phrase

- Let the children look at the melodic shapes on page 7 of the Pupils' Book.

  **B** play

*The notes of these two melodic shapes form the two chords D minor (DFA) and C major (CEG).*

- Hold a xylophone in an upright position so that everyone can see it, and play the notes of each chord, D minor (DFA) followed by C major (CEG), also reminding the children that these are the notes of the two phrases.

D minor 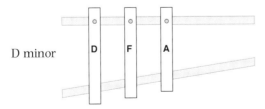   C major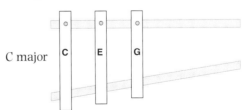

- Ask the children if they notice anything similar about the two chords.
  *(Each chord uses the same pattern of notes.)*
- What do they notice about the starting note of the two chords?
  *(The chord of C major starts one note below the chord of D minor.)*
- Invite the children to sing the whole song again.

# 2: Playing with chords

**Resources**

The Purple Book

Tuned percussion instruments

Keyboards

Recording track 63

**Key vocabulary**

Harmony

Accompaniment

Block **chord**/spread chord

**Previous experience**

Making up accompaniments.

Singing in two parts.

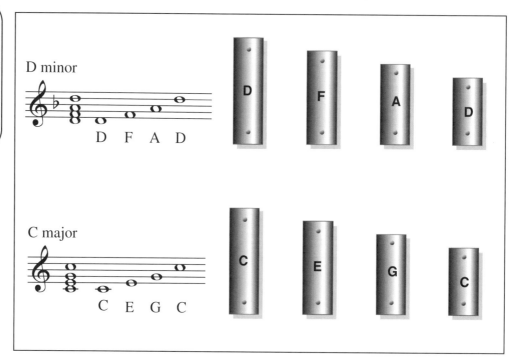

*The Purple Book, page 7*

- Listen to the recording of the second version of 'The drunken sailor' on track 63.

- Ask the children what is different about it. *(Another sung part has been added.)*

The new part is based on the bottom notes of the two chords:

- Ask the children to listen again to the two parts sung together, paying particular attention to the second part.

- Teach the second part to the class.

- Invite half the class to sing the melody, while the other half sing the second part.

*play*

- Ask the children to sit in a circle and place some tuned percussion instruments and keyboards in the circle.

- Invite some children to find the notes of the D minor and C major chords on the keyboards and on the tuned percussion instruments. *(See opposite and page 7 of the Pupils' Book.)*

- Invite individual children to experiment with different ways of playing the two chords. *(With two beaters they can play only two notes, but playing the kind of pattern below taken from a short rhythmic phrase within the song will enable the player to include the three notes of each chord. Likewise some children will feel comfortable playing three notes at once on the keyboard, but others may find it easier to play only two.)*

 *play   sing*

- In groups let the children look at the words of the song, with the chord names of D minor and C major written in, on page 7 of the Pupils' Book.

- Ask the children to try to work out how the two chords might fit as a harmonic accompaniment to the melody. *(They will need to think of the shape and notes of the melody, and will need time to practise the chord changes.)*

- Encourage them to sing the melody and play the chords at the correct place, to check whether or not the chords sound 'right'. *(Remind them that the melody starts on the note A, and circulate amongst the groups to offer help where necessary.)*

 *sing   play*

- Invite the class to sing the shanty, with some children providing instrumental accompaniment. *(Choose different groups to accompany each verse.)*

- Discuss with the children whether they feel it all fits together well.

# 3: Three-chord trick

**Resources**

The Purple Book

A range of tuned and untuned percussion instruments

Recording track 64

**Key vocabulary**

**Chords** I, IV, and V

Chord sequence

**Previous experience**

Recognizing chord changes.

Composing, using a given chord sequence.

## Boogie bass

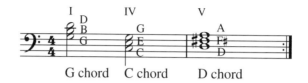

G chord    C chord    D chord

G chord   C chord    D chord

*The Purple Book, page 8*

  *play*

- Set out or mark the three chords of G(I), C(IV), and D(V), as above. The chords are built on the 1st, 4th, and 5th notes of the scale of G.

- Invite three children to play each chord, and label each chord group I, IV, or V. (*Tell the children that musicians usually write the chord numbers in Roman numerals.*)

- Point to each group in turn, so that everyone can hear the three differently pitched chords. (*The notes of each chord should be sounded together.*)

- Invite one child to be the conductor, who decides which chord is played when. (*Changing from one chord to another creates a chord sequence.*)

- Invite other children to take a turn either at playing or conducting, keeping the chord sequences fairly short.

- When you feel that the children are familiar with the chords, ask all the listeners to close their eyes, or turn around so they cannot see the players. Point to one chord group, who play their chord. Can the listeners say which number chord it is? Try with other chords individually. (*Some children will be able to recognize all three.*)

- Repeat the above, but see if they can identify the chords when they are played in sequence. *(Make sure they hear the sound of Chord I before you create a sequence.)*

- Allow a 'conductor' to create a sequence for the children to identify. *(The chord sequence may have to be repeated, so the conductor will need to remember the order of the chords.)*

**B**  *listen*

- Let the children  listen to 'Boogie bass' (track 64).

- Discuss with the children how the piece begins. *(With three chords repeated once. The rest of the tune uses the same notes separated out.)*

- Play track 64 again, and let the children follow the tune on page 8 of the Pupils' Book. *(This piece is based on the chords G, C, and D. As it uses bass (low) notes, it is written out in the bass clef. The children will still be able to follow the pattern of the notes, and any children who have piano, cello, or double bass lessons might be able to work out what notes are used.)*

**C**  *compose*

- Give the groups access to tuned percussion instruments or a keyboard, and make sure all the children know the names and notes of the three chords from activity A.

- Invite the children to experiment with these three chords, playing them in different orders, and deciding on a sequence of four. They might like to look at 'Boogie bass' again on page 8 of the Pupils' Book, to see how that piece was created from three chords.

- Invite them to make up some melodies of their own to fit with their chosen chord sequences, using only the notes of the chords.

- Ask the children to think about some interesting rhythmic ideas, to decide on a structure for their piece, to add some untuned percussion sounds, and some vocals. (These could be sung to made-up words, or spoken, 'rap' style.)

- Invite the children to play and discuss their pieces.

# 1: Creating clusters

**Resources**
Keyboards
Tuned chromatic percussion instruments
Paper and pencils or felt-tip pens

**Key vocabulary**
Cluster
**Chromatic**

**Previous experience**
Using keyboards and tuned chromatic percussion instruments.

Awareness of sharp and flat notes on keyboards and percussion instruments.

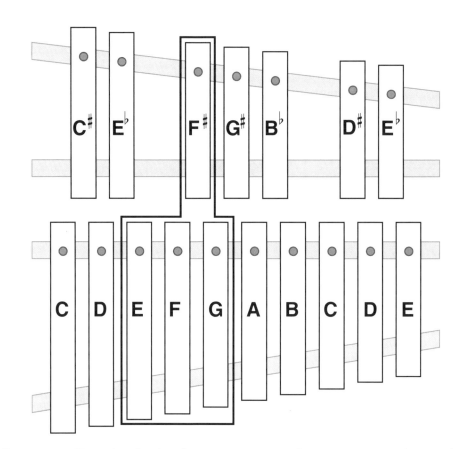

*Composers, like other kinds of artists, continually experiment with new ideas which they incorporate into their work. The idea of using groups of adjacent notes and playing them together is in complete contrast to the familiar use of notes within a scale to make a chord. These groups of close notes, called clusters, create a quite different harmonic sound compared to chord-based harmonies, such as those of 'Drunken sailor' in the previous project. Cluster harmonies can easily be created using chromatic tuned percussion instruments, or keyboards.*

   play

- Set out at least two tuned chromatic percussion instruments and a keyboard. Each instrument should have two beaters.

- Invite children in turn to play the tuned percussion instruments, starting on the lowest C, and playing each bar in turn, going up to the next C, including the sharps and flats.

- Invite another child to do the same (on the keyboard if possible), playing all the black and white notes between the two Cs.

- Explain to the children that they are playing a chromatic scale, that is, playing every adjacent note.

- Invite one child to choose a starting note *(e.g. F)*, and play it on a glockenspiel or xylophone.

- Ask another child to choose a note adjacent to F *(either E or F♯)*, and play it.

- Ask two more children to choose two more adjacent notes, until the children have produced a cluster of four notes, for example those highlighted on page 124.

*To ensure that there is enough room for four players, sit two at either side of the xylophone.*

- Ask the players to enter one at a time, each 'rolling' *(as in a drum roll)* with their two beaters, making a continuous sound to build up the cluster.

- Invite one child to play the same four notes on the keyboard.

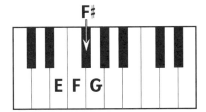

- Ask the player to build up the chord cluster by using a sustained 'voice' from the voice bank *(e.g. strings)*.

  *play*

- In groups ask the children to create one four-note cluster.

- When they have decided which notes to use, ask them to write down the names of the notes *(from the marks on the bars)*, reminding them to use the flat (♭) and sharp (♯) symbols.

- Now ask them to play their cluster notes one after the other, but arranging them in sequences.

- How many different sequences can they make? *(Maximum of 24!)*

- Decide on three or four different sequences to create a short piece.

- Encourage the children to share and appraise their ideas.

# 2: Exploding clusters

**Resources**

The Purple Book

Recording
track 65

Cassette player

Blank tape

Keyboards

Tuned chromatic
percussion
instruments

A range of
untuned
percussion
instruments

**Key vocabulary**

Block/spread clusters

**Previous
experience**

Creating clusters on
keyboards and tuned
percussion
instruments.

*The Purple Book, page 9*

**A** *play*

- Set out one tuned chromatic percussion instrument and one keyboard.

- Ask a child to find and play the lowest D, then the very next note down, C♯.

- Explain that the distance in sound between two notes is called an interval, and that the interval between adjacent D and C♯ is very small.

- Invite a different child to play the low D, followed this time by any C♯ they can find on the instrument, other than the one directly below low D.

- Ask all the children to compare the interval between the first two notes played, and the second two notes. *(The second is a much greater interval.)*

- Now let the children try playing the notes of their chosen cluster very close together *(with small intervals)*, or spreading them over the whole instrument, *(wider intervals)*.

## B compose

- Ask the children to look at the pictures, on page 9 of the Pupils' Book, and discuss how the clusters differ (*e.g. close together, spaced out, exploding*).

- Provide each group with at least one tuned chromatic percussion instrument or a keyboard, and have available a range of untuned percussion instruments.

- Ask them to decide, in their groups, which picture they would like to use as inspiration for a cluster composition.

- They must decide which and how many notes they want in their cluster, and which note they are going to start from.

- Remind them of some of the different ways a cluster can be formed (*e.g. each note entering one at a time in a predetermined order, all the notes being played at the same time, dividing the notes of the cluster over the pitch range of the instruments, so creating wider intervals and a different sound*).

- Encourage the children to add interest and explore variations, (*e.g. by changing the order of the note series, by playing the notes of the cluster slowly and gradually speeding up, by playing the cluster quietly and gradually getting louder*).

- Ask the children to perform their compositions, and record them on cassette.

## C listen

- Play the recording of 'Klavierstücke' ('Piano piece') on track 65, asking the children to listen for musical contrasts, such as:

  short and sustained sounds
  high and low sounds
  notes played slowly and quickly
  notes played separately and together
  sound and silence

- Play the piece again and ask the children to listen for the silent moments. (*To encourage focused listening, they could raise their hands each time they hear silence.*)

# 1: Sumer is icumin in

**Resources**

The Purple Book

Recording tracks 66, 67, and 68

Paper and pencils or felt-tip pens

Xylophone and recorder

**Key vocabulary**

**Ostinato**

Part-singing

Medieval

**Previous experience**

Singing simple rounds and two-part songs.

Using ostinatos.

Su - mer is i - cu - min in,____ lhu - de sing cuc - cu,____ grow - eth sed and
*Sum - mer is a com - ing in,____ loud - ly sing cuc - koo,____ grow - eth seed and*

blow - eth med and springth the wud e - nu.____ Sing cuc - cu.
*blow - eth mead and spring the woods a - new.____ Sing cuc - koo.*

A - we blet - eth af - ter lamb, lhouth af - ter calve the cu. Bul - loc stert - eth,
*Ew - e bleat - eth af - ter lamb, loweth af - ter calf the cow. Bul - lock start - eth,*

buck e - vert - eth, mu - rie sing cuc - cu. Cuc - cu, cuc - cu,____
*buck re - vert - eth, mer - ry sing cuc - koo. Cuc - koo, cuc - koo,____*

wel singes thou cuc - cu,____ ne swik thu na - ver nu.
*well singest thou cuc - koo,____ nor cease thou ne - ver now.*

*The Purple Book, page 10*

- Let the children listen to the version of the song on track 66 (version 1).

- Ask the children what they noticed about the words (*e.g. the strange sounding pronunciation*).

- Let the children look at the old manuscript on page 11 of the Pupils' Book, and explain that English was written and spoken differently in medieval times.

- Let the children listen to the second version of the song on track 67, and discuss the differences.
  *There are now two voices singing.*
  *There is a sung ostinato which starts before the song and this is repeated throughout.*

- Teach them the sung ostinato.

Ostinato 1

- sing cuc - cu

- Play version 2 again (track 67) and ask the children to join in singing the ostinato.

- Play version 1 again (track 66) fading out at 'Awe bleteth'. Help them to learn this first half of the song, singing the medieval words if possible. When the singing is secure, invite a small group of children to add the ostinato.

- Invite one child to play the ostinato on a xylophone or recorder, from page 11 of the Pupils' Book. *(Ostinato number 1.)*

- Let them sing the first half of the song again, with the instrumental ostinato as accompaniment.

**B**  *sing*

- Play the whole of the song track 66 (version 1), asking them to listen for the start of the second half of the song *(at 'Awe bleteth ...').*

- Let them follow the music in the Pupils' Book (page 10) while they listen to the song.

- Play track 66 again (version 1) to help them learn the second half of the song, inviting the children to join in with the recording if this helps them.

**C**  *listen*

- Ask the children to listen to 'Sumer is icumin in', as sung by the Hilliard Ensemble on track 68 (version 3).

- Discuss with the children how this differs from the version they have learned.
  *This version of the song is longer than the first, and it uses more words.*
  *It has a longer ostinato pattern.*
  *It is sung by male voices.*
  *There is more than one person singing; the voices come in one after the other.*

- The diagram below and on page 11 of the Pupils' Book shows how the song is built up into six parts during the performance.

<pre>
              melody 4 _____
           melody 3 _____
        melody 2 _____
     melody 1 _____
  ostinato _____
ostinato _____
</pre>

# 2: Rounds and ostinatos

**Resources**

The Purple Book

Recording
tracks 66, 69,
and 70

The words
of the song

A variety of tuned
percussion instruments

Keyboards

Recorders

**Key vocabulary**

**Round**

**Melody**

**Ostinato**

**Previous experience**

Composing over an ostinato,
as in Project 10, Unit 3.

### Round from 'Sumer is icumin in'

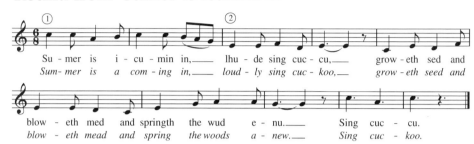

Su - mer is i - cu - min in,____ lhu - de sing cuc - cu,____ grow - eth sed and
*Sum - mer is a com - ing in,____ loud - ly sing cuc - koo,____ grow - eth seed and*

blow - eth med and springth the wud e - nu.____ Sing cuc - cu.
*blow - eth mead and spring the woods a - new.____ Sing cuc - koo.*

**Ostinato 2**

Sing cuc - cu____ sing cuc - cu

*The Purple Book, page 10*

- Revise 'Sumer is icumin in' from page 10 of the Pupils' Book, using track 66 (version 1) to support the revision.

- If the children feel secure with singing the melody, add the ostinato they learnt from Unit 1 (ostinato 1 on page 128). Let the children decide which version of the ostinato to sing and/or play to accompany the song. *(Listen to the balance of the parts to make sure the ostinato is not sung or played louder than the melody.)*

- Play the version of the song on track 69 (version 4).

- Ask the children if they can describe how the song is arranged. *(It is sung as a two-part* round, *accompanied by a treble recorder playing the longer ostinato (see ostinato 2 above) that they heard in version 3 of the song, by the Hilliard Ensemble, in Unit 1.)*

- Form the children into two circles as they did in Unit 1. As they listen to the recording, ask circle 1 to sway when the round starts, and stop when the first part finishes. Circle 2 should start to sway at the entry of the second part, and finish when their part ends.

- Remaining in their circles, let the children sing just the first half of the song as a round, swaying as before as their part starts and ends. *(The second part enters as the first part reaches ②, see above).*

- Rehearse the different entries, making sure that each group comes in clearly and accurately, and that the singing is light and bright.

- Invite some children to add an instrument and/or sung version of ostinato 1 which they heard in Unit 1. It could also serve as an introduction to the round.

**B**   *play*

• Give the children the opportunity to work in pairs to compose their own melody over an ostinato. *(They will need tuned percussion instruments and/or keyboards. Two children can work on one instrument.)*

C   D   E   F   G   A   B   C

• Invite them to improvise their own melodies based on this C scale, over either ostinato 1 from Unit 1, or the longer ostinato (ostinato 2), both on page 11 of the Pupils' Book. Some children may like to create their own ostinato first.

• Ask the children to change over to make sure they have both the experience of playing an ostinato and improvising a melody.

• Invite the children to perform and discuss their compositions with the rest of the class.

**C**   *listen*

• Let the children listen to the extract on track 70, from Benjamin Britten's 'Spring Symphony'.

• Discuss with the children how it demonstrates that old words and a 13th-century melody can be incorporated into a larger and more modern composition.

*extension activity*   *compose*

• Let them record the finished compositions from activity B. *(Recorder and string players may wish to include their instruments.)*

• Suggest that some children write their own 'Summer' poem to accompany the compositions. *(Make sure that everyone is involved, either as players, singers, authors, or readers.)*

# 3: Rap on the move

Pauline Adams

**Resources**
The Purple Book
Recording
tracks 71 and 72

Tuned and
untuned
percussion
instruments
Keyboards

**Key vocabulary**
Rap
Off-**beat**

**Previous experience**
Working with ostinato.
Experimental
vocal work,
as in Project 17.

**Walking down the street**
**Doing it in style**
**Headphones on**
**Music all the while**
**Playing**
**Boom cha boom cha**
**Boom chikka chikka boom**

**Street feet**
**Neat beat**
**Fast track**
**Play it back**
**Boom cha–cha**
**Boom chikka chikka boom**

**Sitting in the bus**
**Head in the music**

**Person sitting opposite**
**No chance to choose it**
**Choos choos sikka sikka**
**Sikka sik choos**

**Running in trainers**
**Logo on cap**
**Pump up the volume**
**It's my kind of rap**
**Rhythm mix**
**Sound fix**
**Techno dance**
**In a trance**
**Boom chikka–ka boom**
**Boom chik chik**

*The Purple Book, pages 12 & 13*

 **A** listen

- Let the children listen to the two different arrangements of the rap on tracks 71 and 72.

- What do the children notice about the accompaniments? *(One version is entirely vocal, with voices used, beat box style, to accompany the rap in a percussive way. The other is accompanied by beat box sounds found on the keyboard, and a repeated melodic ostinato.)*

**B**  *sing*

- Let the children practise saying the rap on pages 12 and 13 of the Pupils' Book. *(You could start with a few voices only, but make sure that everybody keeps together, and watch out for rests (shown opposite as dashes) in the second and last verses.)*

- Ask the children to create a simple beat backing, by clapping on the strong beats:

   x              x            x           x
   Walking down the street \_\_\_\_  Doing it in style \_\_\_\_

- Now ask them to try clicking their fingers on the off-beat:

          x           x            x      x
   Walking down the street \_\_\_\_  Doing it in style \_\_\_\_

- Divide the class into two, one half clapping, the other half clicking, and perform the rap.

**C**  *sing*

- Ask the children to look at the choruses in the rap *(Boom cha boom cha, etc.)*. Are they the same or different? *(Each one is different.)*

- Divide the class into four groups, giving each group one of the choruses.

- Give them time to practise, then listen to each group.

- Invite the children to comment on the performances. *(Were they together? Did they keep a steady beat?)*

- Ask one group to repeat their chorus while the rest of the class says the rap.

- Let other groups try, and if they are successful, try performing the rap with one or more backing groups.

*extension activity*  *sing*

- Let the children try performing the rap as a round, with the second part coming in when the first reach 'Street feet'.

- Ask the children to create their own ostinato-based instrumental or vocal accompaniment to the rap.

# 1: Chinese numbers

**Resources**

The Purple Book

Recording track 73

A range of tuned percussion instruments, set out in the pentatonic scale of C (see activity A below)

**Key vocabulary**

**Pentatonic scale**

Xiaou (pronounced siaow – a bamboo flute)

**Previous experience**

Playing and singing, using the pentatonic scale.

Awareness of different notations.

## Bamboo flute

$$\underline{56}\ \overset{..}{\underline{12}}\ |\ \underline{65}\ \overset{.}{3}\ |\ \underline{52}\ \underline{32}\ |\ 1-\ |\ \overset{.}{\underline{61}}\ \underline{35}\ |$$
Yi – gen    zi – zhu   zhen miao   miao songgei bao bao

$$6\ \ \overset{.}{3}\ |\ 5-\ |\ \underline{65}\ \underline{36}\ |\ 5-\ |\ \underline{65}\ \underline{36}\ |\ 5-\ |$$
zuo   guan   xiao   xiao er dui zhi   kou   kou er dui zhi liao

$$\underline{56}\ \ \overset{..}{\underline{12}}\ |\ \underline{65}\ \overset{.}{3}\ |\ \underline{52}\ \underline{32}\ |\ 1-\ |\ 1\ \underline{13}\ |$$
xiao – zhong chui chu   xue   xin   diao   xiao bao

$$2-\ |\ \overset{.}{\underline{61}}\ \overset{.}{\underline{61}}\ |\ \overset{.}{2}\ \ 6\ |\ 5-\ |\ 1\ \underline{13}\ |\ 2-\ |$$
bao   xudi xudi   xue   hui   liao   xiao bao   bao

$$\overset{.}{\underline{61}}\ \overset{.}{\underline{61}}\ |\ \overset{.}{2}\ \ 6\ |\ 5-\ \underline{6}\ |\ \underline{23}\ \underline{56}\ |\ 5-\ |\ 5\ \ 0\ \|$$
xudi xudi   xue   hui   liao _____

Pronunciation: x = s   zh = j   g as in 'go'

*The Purple Book, page 14*

Chinese music is mainly, but not always, written using the pentatonic scale. It is learnt by using a number system. The dot above a number indicates that it is the same note an octave higher. The dashes underneath indicate two shorter notes in one beat, 0 = a rest. Project 6, Unit 2 also uses a numbered notation.

- Set out the notes of the pentatonic scale starting with C (*the scale of this song melody*), as follows:

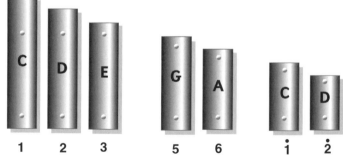

- Ask the children to listen to the pentatonic scale as you play it, starting on the lowest note.

- Play the scale again, asking the children to sing the numbers at the same time.

- Play the scale once more, ascending and descending, asking the children to join in with singing the numbers:

  1 2 3  5 6  1 2  2 1  6 5  3 2 1

- Repeat this activity several times until the children feel secure with both pitching the scale pattern and singing the numbers.

- Play the following short phrases, and ask the children if they can work out the numbers of the notes you played. Let them sing each phrase. *(Before starting to play each phrase, sound and say the number of the starting note.)*

      a) 1 1 1 3 2
      b) 6 5 3 6 5
      c) 2 3 5 6 5

---

(B)  *compose*

- In groups ask the children to make up some pentatonic phrases of their own on tuned percussion instruments, in the same way.

- Let each member of the group have a turn at playing, and everyone should copy, by singing each phrase using the number notation.

---

(C)   *sing*

- Ask the children to listen to version 1 of the 'Bamboo flute' song on track 73, which is sung using the number notation.

- Make sure the children can see the numbered notation on page 14 of the Pupils' Book, and teach them the first half of the song.

- Ask the children if there is any repeated melody pattern, *(6 5  3 6  5  )*.

- Ask what they have noticed about the way the notation is written. *(The quicker notes are grouped in pairs, with a line underneath.)*

- When the children feel secure with singing the first half, learn the rest of the song.

- Ask the children how the second half begins. *(With the same melody as the first.)*

# 2: Bamboo flute

**Resources**

The Purple Book

Recording tracks 73, 74, and 75

A range of tuned percussion instruments, set out in the pentatonic scale starting on C

**Key vocabulary**

Yang-qin (pronounced yang chin – a dulcimer)

**Quavers/minims**

Mandarin

**Previous experience**

Familiarity with the pentatonic scale.

A folk tune from the Han region of China

Young ten-der bam-boo shoot, use it as a flute. Give it to the pre-cious child, pre-cious child, pre-cious child. Young ten-der bam-boo shoot, use it as a flute. Breathe a new song, blow,— blow,— learn to play. Breathe a new song, blow, blow, learn to play my pre-cious_ child._____

*The Purple Book, page 15*

This is a traditional folk song of the Han, who consider themselves the ethnic Chinese people because they were living in China before the Mongolian invasion. They speak Mandarin, which is still the official spoken and written language of China. The song would be sung to a small child and is composed in a flowing, rhythmically uncomplicated style.

- Play the children the recording of the first version of the song on track 73.

- Revise the song, singing the number notation.

- Ask the children to comment on how the song looks when written out in traditional western notation on page 15 of the Pupils' Book.

  *( The paired notes are written as quavers:* bam - boo 6 5 *and the long notes as minims:* flute 1 *)*

- Ask the children to look at the words of the song and the picture of the bamboo flute on pages 14 and 15 of the Pupils' Book.

- Now let them listen to the song on track 74, then sing the song, using the English words. *(The words in a phonetic version of Chinese Mandarin can be found under the numbers on page 14 of the Pupils' Book. These are optional, but there may be someone who can help the children to sing the song in Mandarin.)*

**B** *listen*

- Ask the children to listen to the melody of the song on track 75, played by a concert flute, and a traditional Chinese yang qin shown on page 14 of the Pupils' Book.

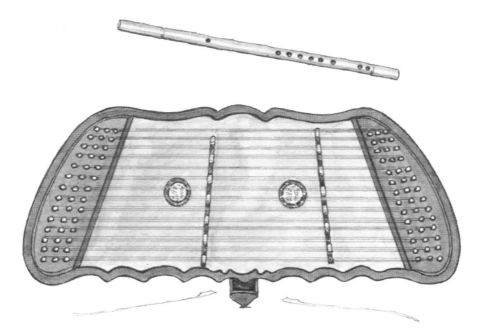

- Ask them if they can hear what the two instruments are playing.
  (*The instruments are playing the melody. Chinese music is mainly in a single line, with no harmony.*)

- Explain that in China, the long notes at the ends of phrases are often decorated to add interest to the music, and that one way of doing this is by 'rolling' the beaters.

- Invite some children to try this technique on the tuned percussion.

- Play the recording again and ask the children to listen for what happens when the long notes are sung. (*The flute plays some extra notes, and the yang qin sometimes plays a fast roll with the beaters.*)

- Let the children sing the song, with some children playing the 'rolls' on the long notes.

# 1: Down the line

### Resources

The Purple Book

Recording tracks
76–81 ☐

Pencils and paper

Four instruments
with bell-like
sounds

**Key vocabulary**

Sound effect

Imitation

**Sequence**

Interpretation

**Previous experience**

Playing and
combining rhythms.

*Sound effects recording*

**(i) Express steam train (track 76)**

**(ii) A local steam train starting out from the station (track 77)**

**(iii) Trains in a marshalling yard shunting wagons (track 78)**

**(iv) A large, busy station (track 79)**

**(v) Sounds inside an old lever-operated signal box (track 80)**

**(vi) Fireman stoking the boiler of a stationary train (track 81)**

*The Purple Book, page 16*

   **A** listen

- Ask the children if they have ever seen a steam train, and if so, where?

- After looking at page 16 of the Pupils' Book, talk about how a steam train works. Can they find out for another lesson what all the labelled parts are for?

- Do they know any stories which feature steam trains (*e.g. Thomas the Tank Engine, The Railway Children*)?

- Ask the children to listen to the sounds of railways and steam trains on tracks 76–81.

- Ask them to describe what they think is happening during each extract. (*See above, and page 25 for details. They may need to listen to the recordings more than once.*)

**B**  *listen*

- Ask the children to listen to the recordings once more, then write down the sounds and events in the order in which they happen. (They can use graphic signs or words.)

- Invite them to compare and discuss their interpretations of what they hear.

- Let them compare their interpretations with what is actually happening in the recordings.

- Are they similar or different?

**C**  *compose*

- In pairs ask the children to imitate, with their voices, some of the steam train sounds.

- Ask them to invent their own sequence of sounds and events, using and incorporating ideas from the recordings *(e.g. trains speeding up, or getting louder and quieter as they pass by)*.

- Let them share their ideas, and ask the listeners to say what they think is happening in each performed sequence.

**D**  *sing*

- Remind the children of the sounds heard on the recording made inside the signal box (track 80, no. v), and the importance of the bell codes in informing the next signal box of an approaching train.

- Invite one child to make up a bell code pattern, using the words 'ding ' and 'dinga', *(e.g. ding ding dinga ding)*.

- Ask the whole group to repeat this pattern.

- Repeat the activity until there are four different bell codes *(e.g. 1. ding ding dinga ding; 2. dinga dinga ding ding; 3. ding dinga–ga ding; 4. ding ding ding dinga)*.

- Divide the children into four groups, giving each group a different bell code pattern.

- Ask the children to stand in a straight row, in four separate lines *(each line representing a signal box)*, then practise sending the four patterns up and down the line.

- Invite one child to be the conductor, to choose and point to one of the four groups. They respond by sounding their bell code *(e.g. bell code 3)*.

- Let the children send the different bell codes up and down the line consecutively, in any direction.

# 2: Clickerty–chuff

**Resources**

The Purple Book

Recording tracks 82 and 83

A range of untuned percussion instruments

Pencils and paper

**Key vocabulary**

**Triplets**

**Waltz**

Symphony orchestra

**Previous experience**

Keeping a steady beat.

Using different rhythms.

*These rhythms may be copied and enlarged.*

*The Purple Book, page 17*

 **A** **play**

- Invite one child to keep a steady crotchet beat by repeating the word 'chuff', whilst another says the triplet 'clickerty', at exactly the same time, so that they keep in time.

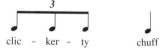

- Divide the class into two, and ask one half to tap the steady beat while the other half says the word 'clickerty'.

- Ask the children, in pairs, to practise this rhythm, both in words and by tapping and clapping.

- Transfer the steady crotchet beat and the triplet rhythm on to woodblocks or claves, or some other suitable untuned percussion instruments.

**B** listen

*A number of composers have written music inspired by the sight and sound of the steam train.*

- Ask the children to listen to the extract from 'Pacific 231' on track 82. *(There is a picture of a page from the musical score on page 18 of the Pupils' Book.)*

- Ask them to listen to the way in which the piece starts. *(The engine is building up steam, ready to move off.)*

- Ask the children what happens to the dynamics of the piece as the train builds up steam. *(The music gets louder — a crescendo.)*

- Ask them to listen to the way the music portrays the train beginning to gather speed. *(This slow, deep-sounding, heavily accented music transmits the idea of the enormous amount of energy needed to move a large steam engine.)*

- Now let them listen to the extract from 'Murder on the Orient Express' by Richard Rodney Bennett, on track 83.

- Ask them to compare the openings of the two pieces. *(They may hear how both composers start their music with the train stationary, then gathering steam.)*

- Play the extract from the 'Orient Express' twice, drawing the children's attention to the little snippets of the main melody which are heard in the opening section. Ask them why they think the composer has decided to keep us waiting to hear the whole melody. *(He might be trying to represent the impatience and excitement of the passengers as they wait for the train to start.)*

- Discuss how effective they think the two composers have been in using all these instruments *(e.g. lots of percussion to emphasize the train rhythms; a variety of low-pitched instruments to convey the strength of the trains; a big sound to convey their size.)* Let them look at page 19 of the Pupils' Book which shows a large symphony orchestra.

 extension activity play

- Some children may be able to work in pairs to develop the rhythms from activity A, as shown in the task on page 17 of the Pupils' Book.

- Other children may be able to perform the rhythms from the notation shown opposite, either straight away or after they have performed the boxed version in the Pupils' Book.

# 1: Night Mail

### Night Mail   W. H. Auden

**Resources**

The Purple Book

Recording track 84

A range of tuned and untuned percussion instruments

**Key vocabulary**

Rhyming

Contrast

**Previous experience**

The rhythm of words.

1. This is the Night Mail crossing the Border,
   Bringing the cheque and the postal order,
   Letters for the rich, letters for the poor,
   The shop at the corner, the girl next door.
   Pulling up Beattock, a steady climb:
   The gradient's against her, but she's on time.

   Past cotton-grass and moorland boulder,
   Shovelling white steam over her shoulder,
   Snorting noisily, as she passes
   Silent miles of wind-bent grasses.
   Birds turn their heads as she approaches,
   Stare from the bushes at her blank-faced coaches.
   Sheep-dogs cannot turn her course;
   They slumber on with paws across.
   In the farm she passes no one wakes,
   But a jug in a bedroom gently shakes.

2. Dawn freshens. Her climb is done.
   Down towards Glasgow she descends,
   Towards the steam tugs yelping down the glade
   of cranes,
   Towards the fields of apparatus, the furnaces
   Set on the dark plain like gigantic chessmen.
   All Scotland waits for her:
   In the dark glens, beside the pale-green sea lochs,
   Men long for news.

3. Letters of thanks, letters from banks,
   Letters of joy from the girl and the boy,
   Receipted bills and invitations
   To inspect new stock or to visit relations,
   And applications for situations,
   And timid lovers' declarations,
   And gossip, gossip from all the nations,
   News circumstantial, news financial,
   Letters with holiday snaps to enlarge in,
   Letters with faces scrawled on the margin,
   Letters from uncles, cousins and aunts,
   Letters to Scotland from the South of France,
   Letters of condolence to Highlands and Lowlands,
   Notes from overseas to the Hebrides
   Written on paper of every hue,
   The pink, the violet, the white and the blue,
   The chatty, the catty, the boring, adoring,
   The cold and official and the heart's outpouring,
   Clever, stupid, short and long,
   The typed and the printed and the spelt all wrong.

4. Thousands are still asleep,
   Dreaming of terrifying monsters
   Or a friendly tea beside the band at Cranston's
   or Crawford's:
   Asleep in working Glasgow, asleep in well-set
   Edinburgh,
   Asleep in granite Aberdeen,
   They continue their dreams,
   But shall wake soon and long for letters,
   And none will hear the postman's knock
   Without a quickening of the heart.
   For who can bear to feel himself forgotten?

*The Purple Book, pages 20–22*

**A** *listen discuss*

- Read as much of the poem as you think suitable with the children *(see pages 20–22 in the Pupils' Book)*, and ask them if they can say in what way the various sections are different.

- Ask the children to tap the pulse as you read verse 3. *(They might notice the difference between those sections that have a regular rhythmic pattern, e.g. 'Letters of thanks, letters from banks', and those that do not.)*

- Ask the children to listen to the poem from the soundtrack of the film 'Night Mail', on track 84. *(Benjamin Britten was commissioned to write his 'Night Mail' music to go with the spoken words of W. H. Auden's poem.)*

- What do they notice about the way it is spoken? *(It might seem strange to the children, but remind them that the film was made about sixty years ago, and styles of speaking change in just the same way as the styles of clothes and music.)*

- Ask the children to listen also to the musical accompaniment.

- Can they hear the 'clickerty clack' rhythm? *(They should be familiar with this, from Project 23, Unit 2.)*

- What do they notice about how the words and music fit together? *(The music carries on between the verses of the poem.)*

**B** *play*

- Ask the children to compose their own music for part of the poem, taking into account its rhythms and changing moods. *(There are various ways in which this can be done:*

  *they could use the whole, or part of, two contrasting sections of the poem, e.g. either sections one and two, or three and four;*

  *they could divide the poem into 8-to-10 line sections, each group working on a different section, so that the whole poem is used.)*

- Ask the children to practise saying the words, and to decide which instruments they want to use.

- Give them time to experiment and sort out their ideas *(e.g. how they are going to balance the words and music so that both can be heard?)*

- Invite them to perform and discuss their compositions.

# 2: Poor Paddy

**Resources**

The Purple Book

Recording tracks 85 and 86

**Key vocabulary**

**Round/canon**

**Ostinato**

**Pentatonic scale**

**Previous experience**

Singing in two parts.

Creating accompaniments.

## Poor Paddy works on the railway

2. In eighteen hundred and forty-two
   from Hartlepool I moved to Crewe,
   and found myself a job to do
   a-working on the railway.
   *I was wearing .....*

3. In eighteen hundred and forty-three
   I broke me shovel across me knee,
   and went to work for the company
   on the Leeds and Selby railway.
   *I was wearing .....*

4. In eighteen hundred and forty-four
   I landed on the Liverpool shore.
   Me belly was empty, me hands were sore
   with working on the railway.
   *I was wearing .....*

5. In eighteen hundred and forty-six
   I changed me trade from carrying bricks;
   I changed me trade from carrying bricks
   to working on the railway.
   *I was wearing .....*

6. In eighteen hundred and forty-seven
   poor Paddy was thinking of going
     to Heaven;
   poor Paddy was thinking of going
     to Heaven
   to work upon the railway.
   *I was wearing .....*

*The Purple Book, page 23*

The melody of this song was originally a sea-shanty, but here it is used as a folk song with words describing the hard life of the Irish people working in England. Many emigrants left the poverty of Ireland, after the failure of the potato crop in 1840, and travelled to England, America, and Canada to start a new life. Often their new life turned out to be nearly as hard as the one they had left. Many of them found work building railways, but they were exploited by their bosses, with poor pay and long hours of work.

*sing*

- Ask the children to listen to the whole song on track 85, and learn to sing it from page 23 of the Pupils' Book.

*The song uses this pentatonic scale*:

- Ask the children to use some or all of the notes of the pentatonic scale to make up some short ostinato accompaniment patterns, using some of the rhythms made by the word patterns in the song, or made-up patterns of their own.

**Examples of ostinato rhythms**

   *sing*

- Let the children listen to the second version of the song on track 86, and ask them how it differs from the first. *(The chorus is sung as a round.)*
- If they feel secure with the verse, try the chorus as a round. *(The second part starts at ② in the music.)*

# 3: *Saying your lines*

**Resources**

The Purple Book

Recording track 87

Paper and pencils

A range of untuned and tuned percussion instruments

Keyboard

**Key vocabulary**

**Rhythmic phrase**

**Melodic phrase**

**Previous experience**

Using sounds and structures to achieve an intended effect.

*The Purple Book, page 24*

**A** discuss

- Ask each group to write down a number of short words and phrases which can be associated with train journeys. The picture on page 24 of the Pupils' Book might give them some ideas (*e.g. places of departure and arrival, platform announcements, the journey itself, and the kind of information given to passengers on the train*).

- Ask them to put their words and phrases into some kind of order (*e.g. Intercity; the fast train; the train is leaving from platform 1; from Leeds to London; calling at Doncaster, Peterborough, Milton Keynes; welcome to British Rail; tickets please; drinks are available at the snack bar; sandwiches, hamburgers, coke and beer; the train arrives at 1900 hours; approaching King's Cross station*).

- Ask the children to decide together how they are going to say the different words and patterns, and then practise them.

- Ask them to divide the different words and phrases among the members of their group, so that each one has one or two lines to say. (*The lines can be repeated as many times as the children wish, e.g. 'Intercity' might be spoken four times before the line 'The fast train' enters. The different speech patterns may also be spoken at different speeds, e.g. 'Approaching King's Cross' could be said much more slowly, to represent the slowing down of the train as it enters the station.*)

- Invite the children to share and discuss their ideas.

**B** *listen*

- Ask the children to listen, on track 87, to 'Different trains', by the American composer Steve Reich. (*He uses speech patterns, vocally, instrumentally, and electronically, and starts the piece with the sound of the train moving quickly along the tracks.*)

- Ask them to tap out the pulse of the music.

- Can they hear how Steve Reich has used the words 'from Chicago to New York' and 'one of the fastest trains' to make up his own speech patterns?

- Can they also hear the instruments playing the rhythms of the words?

*extension activity*    *compose*

- Give each group a range of percussion instruments, and include either an untuned percussion instrument or a keyboard.

- Ask the children to transfer their individual speech patterns on to the instruments. (*They could make up a short melody to fit their speech pattern.*)

- Give them time to work on a group composition which uses one or more of the following musical ideas: speech patterns sounded vocally; speech patterns played on instruments; rhythms which convey the sound of a moving train; train sound-effects made on percussion instruments and the keyboard (*e.g. the train whistle*).

# The big machine

Music and words: Jan Holdstock

# Drunken sailor

**2.** Put him in the longboat
until he's sober,
put him in the longboat
until he's sober,
put him in the longboat
until he's sober,
early in the morning.

**Chorus: Hooray and up she rises ...**

**3.** Put him in the scuppers
with the hose pipe on him,
put him in the scuppers
with the hose pipe on him,
put him in the scuppers
with the hose pipe on him,
early in the morning.

**Chorus: Hooray and up she rises ...**

# *Monitoring and assessing children's achievements*

It is only through practical involvement that children will acquire knowledge and skills in music, and the ability to evaluate their own and other's musical outcomes.

When planning for assessment in music, as in other subject areas, the teacher needs to consider the context and background to the learning. Musical activities should be organized to give children the opportunity to achieve at their current level, as well as offering new and interesting challenges.

Flexibility is important in devising activities appropriate to individual needs. A knowledge of pupils' previous musical experiences, and their on-going progress, will be acquired through whole-school planning, monitoring and recording. To allow for the best possible outcomes, planning and input has to be placed in the context of the school music development plan, and of the wider curriculum, so that the transfer of learning and skills takes place, and children are able to make relevant connections.

Assessment opportunities can be created from observing children at work in both closed and open-ended tasks; listening to what they say; and discussing with them the processes through which their learning takes place. Children should also be given self-assessment opportunities: these can take the form of verbal or written feedback.

Throughout this keystage there will be many opportunities to gather evidence of individual children's achievements. These will arise from the setting of whole-class, small-group and individual tasks, in composing, performing and appraising activities. On-going formative assessment will influence planning and teaching, and will provide a range of evidence for the summative assessment of each child, made at the end of the keystage.

Not every child needs to be assessed on every task. This would be time-consuming and unwieldy for any teacher. Over the keystage each child should be assessed a number of times in a variety of activities, so that a fair overall judgement can be made at the end of the keystage.

## *Singing*

The recorded songs give teachers a number of options. Some will feel happier when teaching a song if supported by the recording, and others, who feel more confident about singing with a class, may choose to learn the songs first and then teach them directly.

All the songs in the book can be sung with or without accompaniment. There are opportunities to add suggested accompaniments, or there is guidance for the children to create their own. The recorded accompaniments are uncluttered and mostly quite simple, so that teachers and children can glean ideas for their own accompaniment arrangements. A variety of instruments are used in the recordings, to familiarize children with the different sounds of a range of different instruments. The use of both male and female voices also allows the children to appraise the different timbres and vocal pitch ranges.

The songs have been chosen or written to complement the musical focus of the projects. Attention has been given to structure, phrasing, and pitch, each song being set into a stylistic, cultural and/or historical context.
The experimental vocal pieces and chants may be a 'way in' for pupils who have little experience of singing and of using the voice. Such vocal work may encourage children to use their voices in a free and experimental way, at the same time giving them opportunities to explore dynamics, tempo, and a range of differently pitched sounds.

When teaching a song, allow the children first to hear the whole song through, so that they can gain an impression of its structure, style, and the meaning of the words. Encourage the children to make some physical response, such as tapping or swaying to the pulse.

Encouraging them to join in at points of repetition, or in a chorus, will familiarise them with parts of the song. Gradually introduce the more difficult phrases and verses. Songs can be revisited over a number of sessions, each time refining a different aspect, for example, clear articulation of words, breathing over phrases, and the use of appropriate dynamics. Sung ostinato parts or rounds may take longer to learn, and parts need to be secure in unison before attempts are made at part singing. Looking at pitch direction and structure will help with memorizing material.

# Music information technology

As information technology extends further into the primary classroom, so the use of music technology should also be integrated into music education. In 1997 the DfEE funded a twelve page leaflet entitled *Primary Music – a pupils' entitlement to IT*. This useful document helps teachers develop appropriate ways of using IT to support their teaching of music, and was written for school co-ordinators of both music and IT. All pages can be photocopied. It is available from NCET, Milburn Hill Road, Science Park, Coventry CV4 7JJ.

### Electronic keyboards

The electronic keyboard is a useful music resource, as it has the advantage of serving as a melody, rhythm, and harmony instrument. It can be used as a solo instrument, or in group work alongside other resources such as tuned and untuned percussion. When buying a keyboard it is useful to consider the following:

- Making a choice between mini-keys and standard-sized keys.
- The pitch range. (Keyboards can range from having 25 notes to 61 notes.)
- The range of different 'voices', some of which imitate other instruments, while others give access to more unusual sounds.
- Facilities for playing set chords by pressing set keys. (For example, automatic chord or arpeggio [spread chord] functions.)
- Whether you would like the keyboard to have a memory so that children can record and store information.
- Choosing keyboards with a transposer control. (The keyboard can then be fine-tuned to the pitch of other instruments, such as a recorder or xylophone.)
- The portability of the keyboard. (To be portable it should have in-built speakers.)
- How robust is the instrument? (Has it lots of buttons that can be pulled off?)

### Computers

Some music computer software programmes give pupils access to composing ideas, working with graphic or traditional Western notation.

Information on musical instruments, composers, and different styles of music is available on CD ROM disks. Access to such programmes and information can support and widen the focus of the work done in music sessions.

# National curriculum requirements

Grids for Scotland, Wales, Jersey and Northern Ireland are available on request from:

Oxford University Press
Music Department
Telephone (01865) 556767 ext 4011

| | Sing | Play | Perform with others | Rehearse and present | Improvise | Explore and organize sounds | Create effects | Record (notate) | Identify instrumental sounds | Identify how music is used | Recognize how music reflects its context | Compare traditions in music | Express ideas and opinions |
|---|---|---|---|---|---|---|---|---|---|---|---|---|---|
| | 5a | b | c | d | e | f | g | h | 6a | b | c | d | e |
| **Project 1 — The Long and the short of it** | | | | | | | | | | | | | |
| Unit 1 Exploring sounds | | ● | ● | ● | ● | ● | ● | | ● | | | | ● |
| Unit 2 Exploring and scoring | | ● | ● | ● | ● | ● | ● | ● | ● | | | | ● |
| Unit 3 Exploring and recording | | ● | ● | ● | ● | ● | ● | ● | ● | ● | | | ● |
| **Project 2 — Feeling the pulse** | | | | | | | | | | | | | |
| Unit 1 Doo-be doo | ● | ● | ● | ● | ● | ● | | ● | ● | ● | ● | ● | ● |
| Unit 2 Patterns | | ● | ● | ● | ● | ● | ● | ● | ● | ● | | | ● |
| **Project 3 — Grouping the beat** | | | | | | | | | | | | | |
| Unit 1 Threes, fours, and fives | | | ● | ● | ● | | | | | | ● | ● | ● |
| Unit 2 Transforming the pulse | | ● | ● | ● | ● | ● | | | ● | ● | | | ● |
| **Project 4 — Answers and echoes** | | | | | | | | | | | | | |
| Unit 1 Hill an' gully | ● | ● | ● | | | | | | ● | ● | ● | ● | ● |
| Unit 2 Call and response | ● | ● | ● | ● | ● | ● | ● | | | ● | | | ● |
| Unit 3 Echo song | ● | ● | ● | ● | ● | ● | ● | | ● | ● | | | ● |
| **Project 5 — Ways with words** | | | | | | | | | | | | | |
| Unit 1 The big machine | ● | ● | | ● | ● | ● | ● | | ● | ● | | | ● |
| Unit 2 Central heating | ● | | ● | | ● | ● | ● | ● | ● | ● | | | ● |
| Unit 3 Machine sounds | ● | | ● | ● | ● | ● | ● | ● | ● | ● | | | ● |
| **Project 6 — Rhythmic vocals** | | | | | | | | | | | | | |
| Unit 1 Monkey chant | | ● | ● | ● | ● | | ● | | ● | ● | ● | ● | ● |
| Unit 2 Gamelan | ● | ● | ● | | | | ● | | ● | ● | ● | ● | ● |
| **Project 7 — Discovering drones** | | | | | | | | | | | | | |
| Unit 1 Droning on | | ● | ● | | ● | ● | ● | | ● | ● | ● | ● | ● |
| Unit 2 Round and round | ● | ● | ● | | | ● | ● | | | ● | ● | | ● |
| Unit 3 Bach and Bartók | | ● | ● | ● | ● | ● | ● | | ● | ● | ● | ● | ● |
| **Project 8 — Building a chord** | | | | | | | | | | | | | |
| Unit 1 Ring out! | ● | ● | ● | | ● | | | ● | ● | | | | ● |
| Unit 2 Tuneful chords | ● | ● | ● | ● | ● | ● | ● | | ● | ● | | | ● |
| **Project 9 — Melody ways** | | | | | | | | | | | | | |
| Unit 1 Oats and beans | ● | ● | ● | | ● | ● | | | | | | | ● |
| Unit 2 Raga moods | | ● | | ● | ● | ● | ● | | ● | ● | ● | ● | ● |
| **Project 10 — Pentatonic patterns** | | | | | | | | | | | | | |
| Unit 1 Zum gali gali | ● | ● | ● | | ● | ● | ● | | | | ● | ● | ● |
| Unit 2 Repeated patterns | ● | ● | ● | | ● | | | | | ● | | | ● |
| Unit 3 Patterns in performance | | ● | ● | | ● | ● | | ● | | | | | ● |
| **Project 11 — Mood music** | | | | | | | | | | | | | |
| Unit 1 Sounds from junk | | ● | | ● | ● | ● | ● | | ● | ● | ● | ● | ● |
| Unit 2 Creating a mood | | ● | ● | | ● | ● | ● | | ● | ● | ● | ● | ● |
| **Project 12 — City music** | | | | | | | | | | | | | |
| Unit 1 The quiet city | | ● | ● | ● | ● | ● | ● | | ● | ● | ● | | ● |
| Unit 2 The wakening city | ● | ● | ● | ● | ● | ● | ● | ● | ● | ● | ● | ● | ● |
| Unit 3 Creation city | | ● | ● | ● | ● | ● | ● | ● | | | | | ● |

**This sheet may be photocopied**

| Project / Unit | Sing 5a | Play b | Perform with others c | Rehearse and present d | Improvise e | Explore and organize sounds f | Create effects g | Record (notate) h | Identify instrumental sounds 6a | Identify how music is used b | Recognize how music reflects its context c | Compare traditions in music d | Express ideas and opinions e |
|---|---|---|---|---|---|---|---|---|---|---|---|---|---|
| **Project 13 Sounds extended** | | | | | | | | | | | | | |
| Unit 1 Trying them out | | • | • | • | • | • | • | • | • | • | • | • | • |
| 2 Time lines | | • | • | • | • | • | • | ◐ | | | | | • |
| 3 Sounds together | | • | • | • | • | • | | | • | • | • | • | • |
| **Project 14 Talking drums** | | | | | | | | | | | | | |
| Unit 1 Dhum tak | | • | • | | • | • | | | • | • | • | • | • |
| 2 Dha dhin dhin | • | | | | | • | | | • | | • | • | • |
| **Project 15 Calypso time** | | | | | | | | | | | | | |
| Unit 1 Panamam tombé | • | • | • | | | | | | | | | | • |
| 2 Bongo rhythms | • | • | • | | | • | | | • | • | • | • | • |
| **Project 16 Twos and threes** | | | | | | | | | | | | | |
| Unit 1 Rhythmic division | | • | • | • | | • | | • | | | | | |
| 2 Cross-rhythm | • | • | • | | | | | | • | • | • | • | • |
| 3 High life | • | • | • | • | | • | | | • | • | | | |
| **Project 17 Exploring the voice** | | | | | | | | | | | | | |
| Unit 1 Comic capers | • | | • | | • | • | • | • | • | • | • | • | • |
| 2 Comic strips | • | | • | • | • | • | • | • | | | | | • |
| 3 Comic voices | • | • | • | | • | • | • | • | • | • | • | • | • |
| **Project 18 Vocal messages** | | | | | | | | | | | | | |
| Unit 1 Chairs to mend | • | | • | | • | • | • | | • | • | • | • | • |
| 2 Street cries | • | | • | • | • | • | • | | • | • | • | • | • |
| **Project 19 Using chords** | | | | | | | | | | | | | |
| Unit 1 Drunken sailor | • | • | • | | | • | | | • | • | • | | • |
| 2 Playing with chords | • | • | • | | • | • | • | | | | | | |
| 3 Three-chord trick | | • | • | • | | • | • | | | | | | • |
| **Project 20 Clustering around** | | | | | | | | | | | | | |
| Unit 1 Creating clusters | | • | • | • | • | • | • | | | | | | • |
| 2 Exploding clusters | | • | • | | • | • | • | • | • | • | • | | • |
| **Project 21 Round up** | | | | | | | | | | | | | |
| Unit 1 Sumer is icumin in | • | • | • | | | | | | • | • | • | | • |
| 2 Rounds and ostinatos | • | • | • | • | • | • | • | | | | | • | • |
| 3 Rap on the move | • | • | • | • | | | | | • | • | | | • |
| **Project 22 Pentatonic melodies** | | | | | | | | | | | | | |
| Unit 1 Chinese numbers | • | • | • | | • | • | | | • | • | • | • | • |
| 2 Bamboo flute | • | • | | | | | | | • | • | • | • | • |
| **Project 23 Steam trains** | | | | | | | | | | | | | |
| Unit 1 Down the line | • | | • | • | • | • | • | | | | | | • |
| 2 Clickerty chuff | | • | • | • | • | • | • | | • | • | • | • | • |
| **Project 24 Train journeys** | | | | | | | | | | | | | |
| Unit 1 Night Mail | | • | • | • | • | • | • | | • | • | • | • | • |
| 2 Poor Paddy | • | • | | | • | • | | | | | • | • | • |
| 3 Saying your lines | | • | • | • | • | • | • | • | • | • | • | • | • |

**This sheet may be photocopied**

# Guitar chords

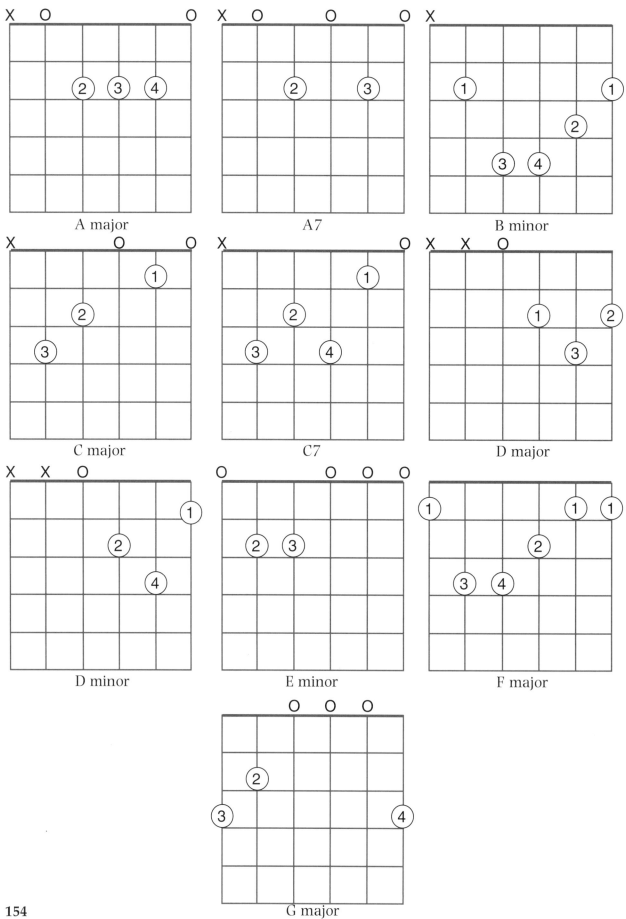

A major

A7

B minor

C major

C7

D major

D minor

E minor

F major

G major

# Blank grid for Project 1, Unit 2

| Name of instrument | 1 | 2 | 3 | 4 | 5 |
|---|---|---|---|---|---|
|  |  |  |  |  |  |
|  |  |  |  |  |  |
|  |  |  |  |  |  |
|  |  |  |  |  |  |

This grid may be photocopied and enlarged.

# *Grids for Project 16, Unit 1*

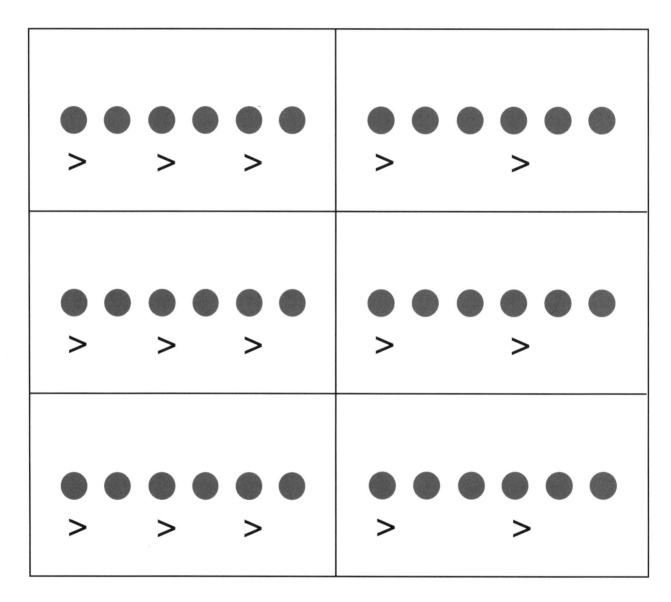

These grids may be photocopied. Photocopy sufficient numbers so that when cut up, each pair of children has six grids, three of each kind.

# Project 16, Unit 2: Cross-rhythm

**Grid 1**

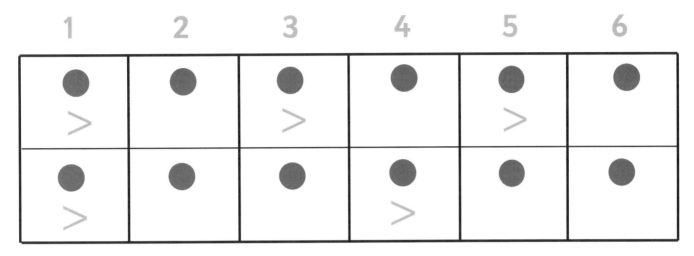

**Grid 2**

This page may be photocopied.

# *Glossary*

**Accent**  Emphasis given to an individual sound, often, (but not always), created by suddenly increasing its volume.

**Alap**  In Indian music, an improvisation on a scale, with a free rhythm, which serves as an introduction to a raga. The notes of the scale are determined by the kind of raga.

**Bar**  Written music is divided into rhythmic units, usually of equal lengths, called bars.

**Bol**  A pattern of mnemonic sounds in Indian drumming.

**Beat**  The throb of a piece of music that you could naturally walk, run or dance to.

**Call and response**  One phrase (the call), sung or played, answered by another.

**Calypso**  Calypsos were originally the traditional oral 'newspapers' of Trinidad and Tobago, the emphasis being on the words, which focus on social and political comment.

**Chord**  Two or more notes of different pitches played together form a block chord. When the notes of the chord are played separately, this is called a 'spread chord' or 'arpeggio'.

**Chromatic scale**  All the adjacent notes within an octave (for example the black and white keys on the piano), played in succession. (E.g. from C to the C above). The smallest step or interval between these notes is called a semi-tone, and there are twelve of these within the octave.

**Coda**  Coda means 'tail', and is an extra bit of music added at the end of a piece.

**Cross-rhythm**  A cross-rhythm is created when two different beat-groupings are played at the same time, (e.g. a 3-beat rhythm and a 4-beat rhythm).

**Damping**  Stopping the vibration of an instrument, either by hand or by placing a felt pad (such as a beater) on it.

**Dhum**  A mnemonic for a low-pitched sound on the darabuka drum. (See also tak.)

**Drone**  A long, continuous sound which stays at the same pitch. Also repeated shorter notes of the same pitch.

**Dynamics**  Variation of the volume of sound: the loudness or quietness of sounds.

**Ensemble**  Two or more performers playing individual parts together. From the French word meaning 'together'.

**Gamelan**  An ensemble consisting mostly of metal percussion instruments, found particularly in Indonesia.

**Glissando**  Playing a number of adjacent notes quickly, either up or down. From the French word 'glisser', to slide.

**Graphic notation**  The use of a variety of invented pictures or visual symbols which are designed to correspond with sounds.

| | |
|---|---|
| **Graphic score** | A piece of music written down using graphic notation. |
| **Improvisation** | Making up music spontaneously while performing it. |
| **Interval** | The distance between two different pitches. |
| **Melody** | A sequence of notes combining pitch and rhythm. |
| **Metre** | The way the regular pulse of a piece falls into groups of two, three, four, or more beats. These groups are written as bars. |
| **Musical score** | Printed or hand-written music which clearly lays out all the parts for each instrument or voice. (Also known as a 'full score'.) |
| **Notation** | Various systems devised for writing down or internalising sounds. (See below for a chart of Western rhythmic notation.) |
| **Note values** | |

| Note shape | Name |
|---|---|
| 𝅝 | semibreve |
| 𝅗𝅥　　　𝅗𝅥 | minims |
| 𝅘𝅥　𝅘𝅥　𝅘𝅥　𝅘𝅥 | crotchets |
| 𝅘𝅥𝅮𝅘𝅥𝅮　𝅘𝅥𝅮𝅘𝅥𝅮　𝅘𝅥𝅮𝅘𝅥𝅮　𝅘𝅥𝅮𝅘𝅥𝅮 | quavers |
| 3　3　3　3 | triplets |
| 𝅘𝅥𝅯𝅘𝅥𝅯𝅘𝅥𝅯　𝅘𝅥𝅯𝅘𝅥𝅯𝅘𝅥𝅯　𝅘𝅥𝅯𝅘𝅥𝅯𝅘𝅥𝅯　𝅘𝅥𝅯𝅘𝅥𝅯𝅘𝅥𝅯 | semiquavers |

| | |
|---|---|
| **Octave** | In Western music this is the interval of eight notes up or down the scale, e.g. from C to the C above or below. |
| **Off-beat/syncopation** | Putting the emphasis or accent on the weak beats of a rhythmic pattern, rather than the usual strong beat. |
| **Ostinato/riff** | A persistently repeated pattern, either rhythmic, melodic, or both. |
| **Part** | A written or memorized line of music for one performer. Each performer in an ensemble or orchestra reads from a part, while the conductor reads from the 'full score' which shows all the parts. |
| **Pentatonic scale** | A scale of five notes, e.g. CDEGA. Pentatonic scales are used within many musical traditions around the world. |
| **Phrase** | A short section of melody or rhythm. |

| | |
|---|---|
| **Pitch** | The highness or lowness of a sound. Pitch is relative to other sounds; for example the sounds of the double bass are lower in pitch than those of the violin. |
| **Pulse** | Pulse is often used as a synonym for beat, though the pulse is a regular and even succession of beats underlying the speed of the music, and is not strong or weak as beats can be. |
| **Raga** | A type of scale in South East Asian music. Each raga has a different series of notes, and often has a particular mood or character. |
| **Rhythm** | Patterns formed by sounds and silences of different lengths. |
| **Round/canon** | Each vocal or instrumental part performs the same music but enters at a different time. |
| **Scale** | A series of notes in ascending or descending order of pitch. |
| **Sequence** | The more-or-less exact repetition of a melodic phrase, but starting on a higher or lower note. |
| **Steps and leaps** | A step is when two notes are adjacent in a melody. A leap is when the difference in pitch between two notes creates a wider interval. |
| **Structure** | The shape of a piece of music. The relationship of one section of a piece to another, e.g. verse and chorus. |
| **Sustained** | A sustained sound is one that keeps going continuously. |
| **Tabla** | A set of two Indian drums, one higher pitched than the other. |
| **Tak** | A mnemonic for a high-pitched sound on a darabuka drum. |
| **Tal** | A time measure used in Indian classical music. Every tal has a set number of beats, which are divided up into groups. (See Tintal.) |
| **Tempo** | The speed at which a piece of music is performed, determined by the speed of the pulse. |
| **Texture** | The texture of music is the quality of sound formed by the different parts. A dense texture is created when there are many parts, a sparse texture when there are few. |
| **Timbre** | The characteristics of sounds that help you to tell one sound from another. |
| **Time signature** | A sign placed at the beginning of, and sometimes within, written Western music. The top number indicates the metre of the music (for example 3, 4, or 5 beat groupings). The bottom number indicates the kind of unit of measurement (for example 4 = crotchet beats, 8 = quaver beats). |
| **Tintal** | A 16-beat time cycle commonly used in Indian classical music. |
| **Triad** | A chord made up of three notes. |
| **Triplets** | Three notes which are to be performed evenly in the time of two. When written in Western notation, a 3 is placed above or below the three notes to indicate that they form a triplet. |
| **Unison** | When two or more people perform in unison, they simultaneously sing or play the same line of music. |
| **Waltz** | A dance which uses a three-beat metre. |